A Dangerous Practice

A DANGEROUS PRACTICE

FALKLAND ISLANDS GP

by

DANIEL HAINES

THE MEMOIR CLUB

© Daniel Haines 2005

First published in 2005 by
The Memoir Club
Stanhope Old Hall
Stanhope
Weardale
County Durham

British Library Cataloguing in
Publication Data.
A catalogue record for this book
is available from the
British Library

ISBN: 1 84104 118 1

Typeset by TW Typesetting, Plymouth, Devon
Printed by CPI Bath

To all the caseworkers of SSAFA-Forces Help (Soldiers',
Sailors', and Airmen's Families Association – Forces Help)
who do so much for those in need.

All profits due to the author from this book are for their work.

Contents

Part IV

List of Illustrations

Foreword

My four months' posting to the Falklands was sudden and unexpected. Just over a year after the campaign I found myself in Stanley with the chance of travelling all over the Falkland Islands. Two things stood out. One was the sheer isolation of the place and its strange beauty. Windswept, with hardly a tree, the climate was extremely variable. The other was the complete devotion of the Islanders to the United Kingdom. Some families had lived there for eight generations. They still took London newspapers and were well aware of what was happening back home, by which they meant Great Britain.

It is worth while reflecting on how we came to be there. It was a place no one wanted. The French, Spaniards and ourselves came and went, until eventually, in 1835, we came and stayed. The nearest country is Argentina and it is as near as Cologne in Germany is to Kent. The Falklands, which is eight thousand miles from the British Isles, is an isolated place.

Daniel and Hilary came to the Falklands after serving as doctors in places such as the West Indies and Swaziland. Daniel, with dental as well as medical training, together with his wife's knowledge of public health and paediatrics, were ideally qualified to act as doctors in the small hospital in Stanley and to make regular forays into the Camp, which was the local expression for the rest of the Falklands. Their love of people, their love of medicine and their love of wildlife were totally fulfilled. Then came the invasion.

With the arrival of the Argentinians their medical skills were more than ever in demand. The invaders thought otherwise and after two weeks they were imprisoned in the Camp. This for them was a shattering experience when there was still so much to do. You will discover from this book much about the key personalities on all sides. The Argentinians do not come out well. Their behaviour was insulting and overnight they imposed their way of life on a population that had been there for one hundred and fifty years. They were freed by, among others, members of the Parachute Regiment. Those tough men showed an understanding and consideration that was exemplary.

I commend this book not least because, you wondered why we went to war over such an isolated place, you will have no doubt, long before the last page, that our action was totally justified.

Paul Abram, Chaplain
HM Tower of London

PART I

An introduction to us and how we ever got to the Falkland Islands in 1980 in the first place

THOSE WHO MOST want peace are those who have experienced war. Those who work hardest to preserve the peace are the military of civilised nations. They frequently lay down their lives for peace. I am sitting in a centuries-old forest on the side of a North Cyprus mountain, under the shade of a pine tree, about two thousand feet up a mountain, overlooking the deep blue Mediterranean Sea. I have just visited the site of the Turkish Army landing on North Cyprus in 1974. I walked among the graves of the soldiers killed, the civilians killed, and the dead, dead, dead military vehicles that they used. Memories of the Argentine invasion of our then home, the Falkland Islands, come flooding back.

Memories fade with time, and in approaching old age, at 61, I want to get some of them set down as accurately but as gently as I am able, before total senility sets in. Twenty-two years ago 'they' came. My precious, tiny, two-table operating theatre was awash with Argentine blood, my wife, Hilary, and I in theatre boots, like wellington boots, paddling around in it. But that comes later.

I was born in 1943 at Hatch Farm, Addlestone, Chertsey in Surrey. The family was evacuated there for the war, my father having had a leg crushed by falling off a bicycle, under the back wheel of an oncoming traction engine, and being found unfit for active service. He taught anatomy to wartime medical students at St Thomas's Hospital. I myself always found anatomy a difficult subject, which I left well alone until I started doing surgery seriously, when it all suddenly became interesting and easy to remember. When I was four years old he was sent to Cairo by the Commonwealth Universities Council to be Professor of Anatomy. I had four happy years there at nursery and infant school, learning what young children learnt in those days – reading, writing, arithmetic – and Arabic as well. I kept chickens, and made friends with Egyptians all over our little area of

Heliopolis, near Cairo. My seven-years-older brother, Ben, developed an interest in history and in chemistry, and made explosives. We had some cracking good times!

Sadly, the family was then sentenced to three years in Sheffield, in the Black Country, in industrial, post-war England. Memory of my teachers at Lydgate Lane Primary School, Crosspool, is of people badly warped by the Second World War. Several were sadists, and took great pleasure in caning us, the young pupils, whenever they could find an excuse to do so. They would be locked up for it now, but they got away with it openly then. Relief! Rescue from the torment of post-war Sheffield. The next appointment was Baghdad, Iraq. The family was there eleven years, and I was with them for the first two, with an amazing education from individual tutors, mainly in a Roman Catholic monastery, at the back of the biggest souk in Baghdad. Can you imagine the sights we saw there? The sounds, the smells? Then, at thirteen-years-old, to boarding school in England. England! A country I only knew from a few home leaves, from tours overseas, and three years in hell in Sheffield. Oh, happy oblivion. The human mind is so good at obliterating the worst assaults of childhood.

So, at thirteen, I was sent to a very free-thinking boarding school, set in 200 acres of its own farmland, on the banks of the River Dove on the Derbyshire-Staffordshire border, where a good emphasis was placed on arts, literature, and debate. But then, as always, there were problems. The headmaster, a highly intellectual Quaker, was a confirmed pacifist. In a debate about the atom bombing of Nagasaki and Hiroshima, I argued fervently that greater good was done by the spectacular and nasty death of a few thousand Japanese than by the slow, tortured death of thousands of Allied prisoners-of-war in their hands. He exploded. 'Damn it, Dan . . .', as I was then called, and the phrase stuck with me for the rest of my school life. He was a wonderful man. He had lost most of his fingers, toes, and another appendage, from frostbite whilst on guard duty during the war. He still took us all swimming, stark naked, in the River Dove, on sunny, summer afternoons. We were all encouraged to walk, to swim, and above all to bicycle around the surrounding beautiful countryside. You can just imagine how that made geography lessons and history lessons come alive. I undertook two projects for O level, the history of church architecture within ten miles of the school, for history, and the sites of pre- and post-Second World War land use by the military for geography. I loved the bicycle rides to visit, describe, and measure these places.

One sadness came from my visits to the old airfields. At one of them the Air Cadets were being given instruction in gliding by regular Royal Air Force airmen. I longed to join them, but my poor, pacifist headmaster just could not contemplate one of his beloved pupils working with the Royal Air Force. He said no. The effect of his refusal? In my freshman week at university, I immediately joined the University of London Officers' Training Corps. I remember today the raised eyebrows of my interviewing officer, Colonel Cahill, when he asked me what school I came from . . . but they desperately needed medical and dental recruits in those days. The cold war was at its height so, for their sins, they took me on and trained me as a soldier. When I was commissioned they told me to organise a reception for Her Majesty the Queen Mother at our officers' mess. It went very well. She was, as ever, extremely pleasant, gracious, and encouraging to us all. It was a great success, with champagne and roses unlimited. Her Majesty left. We cleared up, but there was a huge quantity of champagne left over, and the beautiful roses would have gone to waste. We helped not to waste the champagne, then each of us went home with a large bunch of roses for our girlfriends. I ended up bicycling home at one in the morning, in full Blues (formal ceremonial uniform), with an enormous bunch of roses on the back carrier of my bicycle, where I normally carried my textbooks. I was very, very drunk. Somehow, I shall never know quite how, the road home and the steps up to the front of St Paul's Cathedral became inextricably confused. I found myself pedalling along a long step, getting ever further and further above the road I wanted, which was sloping down away from me. A very large policeman walked slowly up to my step, and stood there. He asked in his posh, brass-buttoned voice of authority what I thought I was doing. What he thought of my explanation, that I had been entertaining Her Majesty Queen Elizabeth, the Queen Mother, he did not share with me. He was very polite, and firm that I should return to the road, and sent me, and my roses, on to home and to bed.

CHAPTER 2

Student days

I SPENT ELEVEN YEARS at the University of London, studying first dentistry, then medicine. I came out with a string of post-nominal letters longer than my name, and the start of a career in forensic medicine. As my father had a series of jobs around Africa and other none too stable countries, my parents kept a large family house in south-east London, not too far from Guy's Hospital, where I studied. I lived in one part of it, and let the rest to fellow students to supplement my grant. I continued in the University of London Officers' Training Corps (OTC), and led the medical section. Life was full of very attractive young ladies. I had seven regular girlfriends, one for each night of the week. Then I met another, and I really fell for her. Difficult. So I invited the original seven to Sunday lunch, left plenty of food and cider for all of them, and went out myself, with number eight. I did not see any of those seven again for over a year, and when I did they were none too polite, but they did have a good Sunday lunch.

The OTC arranged a Regimental Dinner at the Royal Artillery Mess at Woolwich, a long, formal dress do in a brilliantly lit hall, full of regimental treasures and gleaming silver. Very, very posh. My new, smart, best girlfriend was to come to the dinner as my partner. The day before the dinner she told me to go and get lost. She had found someone much nicer. I was distraught. All my Army friends were expecting to meet this gorgeous number eight (alas, senility has caused me to forget her name) and she had ditched me. Well, one of the fellow students renting a part of the family house was a lovely medical student called Hilary. I asked if she would bail me out and she said yes. She came in a magnificent, shimmering, green ball gown, and was a huge success. We have been married thirty-six years now.

We both qualified, and started our careers, mine in forensic medicine, and hers in public health. We had a fine baby boy, and named him Tudor, very Welsh, after Hilary's father. We followed the medical strategy: 'Early to bed, early to rise, work like hell, and advertise.' I wrote a string of learned papers on forensic dentistry. I was doing full-time work in pathology, examining specimens of blood, urine and faeces to detect the causes of disease in hospital patients. I learned the art of doing post-mortem examinations on the patients who died. Useful, this. You can really study what went wrong with the patient, and their treatment, and why they died. You can see how well, or badly, any operation has been done, and judge the surgeon accordingly, which puts you in a strong position. In forensic post-mortems you study how the patient died, or was killed. I was beginning not to have such a wonderful time. My first professor married one of the forensic haematologists (blood studies), and died suddenly and mysteriously. His successor, a furiously hard-working and fun-loving Scot, had a very severe heart attack. My best friend in the Forensic Pathology Department worked too hard, lost his marriage, and went and took a massive overdose in his car. They found his body two days later. Whose turn next?

We had our second baby, a beautiful little girl. We called her Catherine, after my very first childhood sweetheart. The original Catherine, aged eight, and I kept caterpillars. She collected leaves for them. We got very good at it, and raised most through the chrysalis stage to adult butterflies. It was a lovely relationship. She knew her caterpillars, Catherine did. So there we were. Family. Careers. Suicide and Death. I went to see Hilary, in the post-natal ward. She was nursing the new Catherine at the breast. I said, 'I have had enough of this work. All my patients are corpses, many of which have died a very unpleasant death. I spend most of my day with blood, urine and faeces. Let's go and do something else.'

'Yes', she said. 'I would rather you were not the next one. Let's both go and be GPs overseas.'

This response surprised me a bit. We had had a two-month working visit to Ghana, in West Africa, when I had studied children's medicine, and Hilary public health. We had seen some amazing sights. A chief's wedding, kwashiorkor, crude rum being made . . . but that is another story. So we looked at the advertisements at the back of the *British Medical Journal* – it was all in one in those days – and there was the Overseas Development Administration of HM Government advertising for doctors to be seconded to the Government Hospital, the Seychelles. We read all we could find about the Seychelles Islands, and applied. At the interview, a splendid old doctor left over from the Colonial Medical Service days said, 'Sorry, those jobs went months ago. Long before the advertisement came out. How about the

Cayman Islands?' I said that I had never heard of them. Were they in the Pacific?

'No, no. They are in the West Indies. Go and give it a go!'

We went off and read all we could find about the Cayman Islands. There wasn't much. A tax haven. Lots of banks. Tourism. Hotels. But the people? Oh dear, dear, dear. These used to be pirate islands. Nearly all the population was descended from pirates, highwaymen, robbers, murderers, and the slaves of this motley crew. Add to this rich mix the present-day pirates, the off-shore bankers, and you really have an intriguingly corrupt population.

We also discovered when we arrived there that there was no income tax, cheap alcohol and a predilection for drinking ganja (marijuana) tea. I was in the little casualty room one Sunday afternoon. A six-foot, seventeen-stone lady had been to church and had been drinking ganja tea, laced with rum. She was a little high, and took it into her mind to pirouette, right there in our little casualty room. Round she went, faster and faster, and ever faster, as trays of instruments and trolleys got caught up in the whirlwind. She gathered momentum like a giant flywheel, her huge bust adding to the mass of the disastrous equation. There was nothing we could do except move anything we could to safety from this ferocious female whirlwind. Suddenly it stopped and it was all hands on deck to remove this large, unconscious body from our casualty floor to a hospital bed. There was no apology next morning, just 'It was a church tea party, doctor!'

CHAPTER 3

Cayman Island life

WE ARRIVED ON Grand Cayman, via Miami, at around midnight – Hilary and myself, Tudor, just two years old, and Catherine, three months. The anaesthetist met us with the hospital minibus, and off we went to a beachside hotel for our first night. It had been a hard day – eight hours' flight from London to Miami; kept under armed guard there until our flight to Cayman; wrong information from the US embassy that visas were not needed for transit, so we were illegal immigrants in Miami for two hours; relief that we were on the final leg of the journey. Such relief that I started to vomit. Or was it the Miami drinking water? Whatever, the anaesthetist wanted to admit me immediately to the hospital. I told him where to go, lay down, and slept.

I was woken by the tropical sunrise over the sea at six next morning. The family were deeply asleep. I had a very empty stomach, having lost the entire contents the previous night. This was a holiday island, and we were in a beachside hotel. There must be food around somewhere. No way. Breakfast was due at nine, and not a minute before. So I walked a mile into Georgetown, the capital, and bought enough food for all of us. The family woke and loved it. The hotel manager sent breakfast for all of us at nine, and we sent it back, suggesting he pay for my purchases. That day we went off to a very attractive bungalow, our home for the next two years. There was a large garden all around and I got back to keeping chickens. The damned dog from over the road ate one of them. I kicked the dog. The lady of the dog's house said, 'Dr Haines is a very wicked man.' Right in one! (says Hilary).

At the hospital, we had really struck lucky. This was a training post. Harry McGladdery, Fellow of the Royal College of Surgeons of Ireland, took his teaching very seriously with all five doctors there. We each presented cases from our previous week's work, discussed how we had handled them, and what had gone right and what had not gone well. I did the post-mortems, so usually had the last say. It was a quick way to learn. He found us serious students. He

9

demonstrated every surgical case he had before he operated – the signs to look for, the tests to do, making quite sure we could tell a direct from an indirect inguinal hernia, how to tell an infected appendix from a fallopian tube full of pus, how to reduce an 'irreducible' hernia by the correct suspension of the patient, legs up. All good, practical stuff. Whenever he operated he had me in, either as assistant or as anaesthetist. I had had a very good anaesthetic training whilst in the Territorial Army, where I was taught by two Regular Army consultant anaesthetists, and then did locum and weekend cover for their juniors. The old military hospital was not far from home. The official Cayman hospital anaesthetist didn't think much of my usurping his place, for I was meant to be just the GP and the junior obstetrician. But he was over-fond of sailing with his beautiful, languid wife around the island, so he could seldom be found when he was wanted, and I got in the valuable experience.

Dr Peter Wilkinson, Member of the Royal College of General Practitioners, took an equal interest in our education. He was in charge of general medicine, and obstetrics. He had an Australian passport, while Harry was as Irish as they come. Peter had a large white Mercedes car, of which Harry was a bit jealous, whereas Peter, as second in command, was a bit jealous of Harry's status, salary, and beautiful house, worth a cool million today. But they both taught and taught. I became confident with obstetric forceps, and learnt the skills and pitfalls of anaesthetics for Caesarean section operations. Our time there was coming towards the close. Among our patients were fifteen scientists and specialists who worked for NASA in a space tracking station on Swan Island, 400 miles away. Our old Dakota flew supplies out to them once a fortnight. They would come to Cayman to relax. One Swan Island scientist came for a fortnight's holiday swimming and snorkelling around the coral reefs. He was quietly snorkelling off the beautiful, soft, white, coral, sandy, seven-mile beach when a speed boat passed over his legs at full power. He received eight huge, deep salami-slice cuts across both thighs. I was alone in the casualty when they brought him in. We sent urgent calls for Harry to come, but he wasn't found for hours, so I settled down to repair him myself, slice by slice – three hours of rather precise sewing. No major arteries or nerves had been cut, but plenty of small ones. Hilary kept both my and the patient's spirits up, keeping him well anaesthetised with local anaesthetic as I sewed along, and telling him that his legs looked lovely.

As I was on the last gash, Harry came in, took a long hard look at what I was doing and told me to carry on and finish it off. He was delighted. His teaching was paying off. The patient made a brilliant recovery, and was back to sport in a few months. We, the whole family and a visiting medical student friend, were all invited to Swan Island for a day. The five of us, and a few stores, had a twenty-eight seat Dakota aircraft all to ourselves. Tudor, now nearly four, made most of both flights sitting on the pilot's lap. I rode in the third (middle) seat, between pilot and co-pilot. On arrival at Swan Island you do a low pass over the grass airstrip, and the shepherd boy runs out with a long pole, and chases all the cows off the field, then you come round again, check there are no cows in the way, and land with a few feet to spare. We had a wonderful day. So many things happened on the islands that I would love to write about, but that's another story. We were judged fit to practise on our own in obscure places. Hilary was pregnant again, with our third, and last child, conceived in Cayman. It was all great fun.

CHAPTER 4

Swaziland

To know what you do not know is important in medicine. Toward the end of our time in the Cayman Islands I realised I needed a lot more training in obstetrics, gynaecology, and the care of premature babies. We took eight months off from our travels for me to work on this, and for Hilary to write up her thesis on her work in the Cayman Islands, on child growth and development there, and to have our third baby.

It all worked remarkably well. I got a six-month job doing obstetrics and gynaecology with two really keen consultants at Greenwich District Hospital, on the meridian. Then I satisfied the examiners, as they say in the letter telling you that you have passed the diploma examination. A severe case of multiple diplomatosis, mine. We both then had an amazing few days at the Margaret Pyke contraception training centre, learning more about fitting coils, the wonders of the female hormonal system, and pills. We learnt there are more colours, shapes, sizes and flavours of condoms than we had ever dreamt of. Then I did two weeks in a premature babies unit. Getting intravenous drips up in a premature baby is a bit like threading a very small needle with your eyes shut. I did, and still do, hate the job. Hilary got her thesis well under way. One of my consultants, Eric Barnard, delivered her of our third child, our second son, Gwyn, after his Welsh uncle, a rudely healthy baby boy, who yelled so loud at birth that he was ordered out of the delivery room whilst the staff tidied up.

So we were ready for off again. Botswana was on the list. We read up all about it and applied. The splendid old Colonial Service doctor had retired, only to be replaced by another one of the same species.

'Yes, Botswana? Sorry, old chap. Job's gone. How about Swaziland?'

We were delighted. Only about 500 miles out this time. I even got to recce the place at their expense. A huge man-made forest, twenty-five miles square, was to be our patch, with the Great Usutu River running through the centre and the forest all on mountains.

12

There were villages and settlements at all heights from 2,000 to 7,000 feet in the forest, and a giant paper pulp mill and township in the middle, on the river. Our home, a beautiful bungalow with polished wooden floors, stood at 6,000 feet up in the mountains. There was an open hearth log fireplace in the living room, with free firewood, and a first-class English-type primary school one mile away.

I worked full time, Hilary part time, until our new baby, Gwyn, was a bit older. We had plenty of help with our house, huge garden, and with the children. I got back to keeping chickens, and geese and ducks this time. A neighbour's dog killed one of the ducks but this time I did not kick the dog. I took the dog on a rope lead, and the dead duck for evidence, and left them both there with a rather bemused policeman. The neighbour was later heard muttering things about mad dogs and mad Englishmen, in Afrikaans. I told the policeman he could eat the duck.

It was my first real command. I was the Chief Medical Officer, with Hilary and fifteen well-trained nurses to help me. My instructions were to provide a general medical service to all 12–15,000 people living and working in the forest, and to prepare for eventual 'localisation' by teaching the local people to take over and run the show wherever possible. I had a generous, but strictly limited, cash budget to do this, about a third of a million pounds a year. The vast majority of this went on staff salaries and wages.

Our strategy was to teach the fifteen nurses to do most of the normal work of an English general practitioner and to teach the dozen or so ancillary workers to run the laboratory and preventive health care service. Two of our nurses, of whom one was a trained physiotherapist, were already well trained in X-ray work and they taught us a lot. We carried on the excellent tradition of weekly teaching sessions for all staff, but this time we were the instructors, they the students. We had a fully-equipped twelve bed GP hospital and we did everything, other than major surgery and complex laboratory investigations, on the spot. There was an American consultant surgeon twenty-five kilometres away, down a very rough dirt track, in Mbabane, the capital. He did our major surgery, with me assisting. He and some of the other staff helped with some of the teaching in our hospital too.

We were high in the mountains, well above the malaria and bilharzia zones, but our patients often came from the lower zones, so we saw plenty of both. We also became very familiar with tuberculosis, leprosy, gonorrhoea, syphilis, worms of every length and shape, as well as all the usual illnesses that make up general practice anywhere in the world. We also met up with a magnificent array of the rarer venereal diseases. The Gordon Highlanders had been in Swaziland ten years earlier to quell an uprising. They were accredited, fairly or unfairly, with leaving every variant of venereal disease known to man behind them, along with an awful lot of mixed-race babies. We learned to diagnose typhoid fever from the temperature chart and the smell on the patient's breath long before the laboratory diagnosis was confirmed. A baby girl died in my arms, from measles, as I held her for initial assessment. I have been a bit hot on measles immunisation ever since.

A white South African long-distance lorry driver came to the hospital with a 'wazzit on his wazzname', as the nurse delicately described it – a great big primary syphilitic ulcer on his penis. I told him what it was. 'Impossible,' he said. 'I have never slept with a black woman.' I informed him that syphilis does not follow the rules of apartheid. He was genuinely shocked. It was a magnificent ulcer!

Whilst in Swaziland I missed the Anglican Church. The nearest was twenty-five kilometres down that dirt road, so I and a few like-minded people started to say matins or evensong together in the beautiful thatched multidenominational church in the nearby village. The bishop, Bernard Mkhabela, was delighted, and more or less told me to do some part-time study in theology. I was ordained deacon in the second year.

Hilary was a huge success with the families. An experienced mother of three herself, she established a powerful primary care service for families throughout the forest. On one occasion she found a formal notice on the front door of her main clinic building – 'The Inyanga of Bunya' (The Witch Doctor of Bunya). She had arrived! To my regret, she made them take it down.

Three years in Swaziland did not seem long enough. So what next?

PART II

CHAPTER 5

Life at peace in the Falkland Islands

THIS TIME we actually went where we had expected to go – the Falkland Islands. The five of us, the children aged eight, six and three-years-old flew out from Gatwick to Buenos Aires in the Argentine in a spacious Tristar. We spent three days in an ancient colonial hotel, where we waited hours for meals and the waiters put on a Laurel and Hardy act each time they brought in an item of cutlery or a dish through the huge heavy rotating doors from the kitchen. The food was overcooked, tasteless, and almost inedible. We made visits to the Argentine hospitals, where all assured us of their very best services, but we already knew that the Falkland Islanders ('Kelpers', from using kelp, the giant seaweed that grows round the islands, often eighty feet long and a foot wide, as fertiliser and to make agar gel for biology laboratories and ice cream) would prefer not to send a sick sheep there, let alone go themselves. They did not like or trust the Argentines.

We paid a short visit for lunch with a chaplain to the Mission to Seamen. He was not a brilliant cook. I told him I thought the fish was nice. It wasn't. It was overcooked chicken. He offered me a gin. I declined. He poured his own, a huge glass, full to the top. No tonic. No wonder he managed to murder the chicken. He was a very nice, jovial man, and gave us the one meal we could enjoy at all in those three days. I hope he forgives my rudeness about his chicken.

Then on south, over Patagonia, in an Argentine military plane, towards the cold south, subantarctic regions.(The cold south. The world is upside down there. OK? The moon is upside down there too). Last refuelling at Comodoro Rivadavia, a huge military oil refinery wasteland, and then up and over the 300 miles of South Atlantic Ocean to our new home. On arrival, customs and immigration was all one man, Toddy, the charming senior policeman, who had a staff of three constables. That's how he introduced himself, Toddy. And a more helpful police officer I have yet to meet. More of that anon.

★ ★ ★

We were met by the outgoing Senior Medical Officer, a short man, who greeted us with a clear statement that he was appalled that I had been appointed to replace him. How could I possibly replace a doctor as smart as him? He took against Hilary too. He did not like women at all. He loathed women doctors. And tall women terrified him. Hilary is all three! He left a few weeks later to become quite a respectable eye surgeon, so I hear. I suppose you don't have to worry too much whether an eye is male or female.

So we left the airstrip, wondering what we had let ourselves in for this time, and on to lunch. The chaplain and his wife, Harry and Iris Bagnall, had invited us to have our first meal on the islands with them. It was a little strained – grace, roast mutton and a long lecture on the hardships of living there. We had to grow our own vegetables. (I happen to be a very keen gardener.) We had to keep our own fowl if we wanted eggs or chicken to eat. How burdensome! (If there is one thing I really enjoy, it is keeping my own fowl. I still do, even in London.) I had to wear black shoes whenever I went to the cathedral. (I never did quite understand that one. Doesn't God like brown shoes?) And anyone who wasn't a proper Christian was damned. *I am the way, the truth and the light. There is no other way but through me.* We couldn't take that. We are sound Anglicans, but we have a deep respect for the rich tapestry of other religions of people seeking after God. I cannot see God damning other people because they are not 'proper Christians'. So there we had to agree to disagree. Not an auspicious start. From the vicarage we went to our new home, a real beauty this time – a two-storey house, set in nearly two acres of gardens and grass paddock, overlooking the harbour.

The house was built of wood, by a master carpenter from the British Antarctic Survey (BAS) organisation. It had two floors, plus a huge attic, oil-fired central heating, mains electricity and water. There were beautiful carvings of sheep, and the Islands' crest, on the doors of cupboards, and there was lots of space, warmth and comfort for all of us. The outhouses were a treat, for there were two spacious garages, previously horse stables, and we had a brand-new long-wheelbase Land-Rover and a Mini City. There was a very large workshop shed, with everything necessary for carpentry, and plenty of space for a large deep freeze, as well as another sizeable stable for horses, which we did not have, and which we used as our main chicken run. There was a hothouse-greenhouse, with a peat boiler at one end, and under-soil hot water pipes from this all around, which meant tomatoes, broccoli and courgettes for us. There was a Wendy House for the children,

A picture of our house taken from the Beaver float plane as we landed.

The view from home.

which they loved and in which they plotted all their mischief. They made a one-mile cycle ride along the harbour front to school each day.

The gardens were great, with formal front and side gardens, and a large sloping lawn, which was lovely for children to play on in the sunshine. I enriched the very large vegetable plot with Land-Rover loads of kelp, that rotted down to a rich manure for all the greens and root crops. The paddock of over an acre, on which to keep the horses that we did not have, was excellent for ducks and geese, which made a lovely change from the all-prevailing mutton. It was hard physical work, but I loved it. I was up at six each morning to rake out yesterday's peat in the hothouse boiler (the ashes make a useful fertiliser), build up the boiler for the day, adjust the sprinkler and ventilation to suit the day's weather and feed the fowl. Our nearest neighbour was Dick Baker, the Chief Secretary and Deputy Governor, and he had precisely the same routine. We both did most of these domestic chores in our pyjamas in the summer months, and felt a sort of working comradeship. The Bakers had two very attractive young daughters, who became inseparable from our three. Mrs Baker was a very good mother to all five children when they invaded her house.

Soon after our arrival, the Governor's wife, a lady whom I found a little difficult at times, came to visit Mrs Baker, and found our three-year-old, Gwyn, observing her carefully from under a bush. She demanded of him, 'And who are you?' He is reported to have come out from under the bush, stood up to his full height, and replied, 'I am Gwyn Daniel Hugo Haines. And who are you?' Ask and you shall receive!

CHAPTER 6

The King Edward VII Memorial Hospital

THE WALK TO the hospital was one kilometre along the harbour wall. Immediately outside our front gate was the hulk of an old sailing ship, a three-masted East Indiaman, the *Jhelum*. It had been converted by BAS into a wood workshop, from which our house, among others, had been built. We could sit on the far side and fish for grey mullet, a useful, if undistinguished, fish, not half as good as the sea trout you could get just up the river. The walk along the harbour wall was nearly always accompanied by a giant petrel, or 'stinker', named for the perfume of their fish foul droppings. The size of eagles, they loved to hover over people and cars as they passed along the harbour wall.

In the hospital gardens, food was grown by Abbie, the gardener, for the hospital patients and the live-in nurses. Mutton and milk were delivered daily, but even the hospital had to grow its own vegetables and produce its own eggs. The cook, an Anglo-Argentine, was unimaginative. We did not envy the patients or nurses their food.

We had eleven acute beds in four small wards, each named after a ship or admiral involved in the great World War battles of the Falkland Islands. *Cunningham. Ajax. Exeter.* There was a three-bedded maternity ward, with adjacent delivery room and ten beds in the older, wood-built part of the hospital as a sort of old people's home. The operating theatre was on the smallish side, with one standard table, and a second, less well-equipped table near it. We also had a very good overhead light, a good, modern anaesthetic machine, and a decent ventilator. Oxygen and nitrous oxide cylinders came on the quarterly supply ship from England. As we did rather a lot of surgery, we soon ran seriously short of bottled oxygen, but we did have three 'Cardiff oxygen concentrators' which give about 40 per cent oxygen from the atmospheric air. All three, two in parallel, and the third in line, gave enough oxygen to run the anaesthetic machine efficiently. This machine added nitrous oxide (laughing gas) and a good dose of the anaesthetic agent halothane to the oxygen delivered to the patient via the ventilator, and kept the patient happily anaesthetised for hours, without wasting our precious oxygen cylinders.

The X-ray department was very well equipped, with full facilities for standard X-rays and for barium studies. The laboratory was also fully equipped for all standard tests and studies, with a very able technician running both. I felt I was back to blood, urine and faeces again! Sort of home from home. We divided our duties. Hilary did all the paediatrics, anaesthetics, school and public health medicine, and preventive medicine. I did the surgery, obstetrics, and radiology. We shared the gynaecology, family planning, and general practice. We had five qualified nurses, and six unqualified auxiliaries. One of the qualified nurses was local, a Kelper, and was very good indeed. We trusted her. And there was Robert Watson, the dental surgeon.So we had a really good staff for most jobs. The testing times came when we had a Caesarean section to do. You really need an anaesthetist, a surgeon, an assistant surgeon, and a skilled paediatrician if the baby needs help getting started. Help was not at hand. Hilary had to be both anaesthetist and paediatrician at the same time, and I had to make do with a nurse assistant.

Soon after we arrived a young man overturned his tractor at speed. The glass windshield shattered, and he had over a hundred little cubes of windscreen glass in his face, neck and shoulders. I asked Robert, the dentist, to come and help us. He proved himself to be a superb operator, keeping his calm throughout. Between the three of us we removed every piece, and sutured every wound, within a couple of hours. Thereafter Robert always joined us at surgical operations and extended his dental skills to appendicectomy, and to be first assistant at Caesarean sections, whilst Hilary looked after the anaesthetics and the baby resuscitation. All did well every time. What a team!

Robert had a well-equipped dental surgery. He also had his own sturdy sailing boat, which had been an admiral's barge. That is a small boat that is carried on the deck of the admiral's flag ship, his warship whence he commands the fleet, that could be lowered into the water for him to visit and inspect other ships of his fleet. In summer, Robert and his wife would load all his dental kit, and a foot-powered dental drill, into his little boat, and sail around the thirty odd settlements outside the capital cathedral village of Stanley, and check and repair every inhabitant's teeth or dentures. His wife was a great sport, and supported him totally. They were both Baha'is, a gentle, pacifist, inclusive religion. I thought they were as close to God as anyone,

Round the world yacht. One of the many small sailing ships that called into Stanley for repairs and victualling.

certainly myself, but in the chaplain's mind they were damned to everlasting torment in Hell. They kept their picturesque white-painted boat moored on our side of the *Jhelum*, an artist's dream. From our front sitting-room window we looked over our sloping front lawn, over the road, to both the little sailing ship and the East Indiaman.

Back to the hospital. There was also a post-mortem room, or brick shed, at the back of the hospital, which was small, but sufficient. Post-mortem instruments are much the same as surgical instruments, but are generally larger, as finesse is not the order of the day. Most of the instruments in that room were actually from the old ships of the Royal Navy that had taken part in the two major naval battles around the islands in the two World Wars, the Battle of the Falkland Islands, and the Battle of the River Plate. I can only imagine that the ship's surgeons had come ashore to do their post-mortem examinations in the hospital mortuary, and in their personal distress in doing that last, final examination of their friends, colleagues, and brothers-at-arms, had forgotten to take their instruments back with them. I feel deeply for them.

The Senior Medical Officer's room was the grandest in the building. My secretary, Shelley, sister to one of the island's four police constables, and I had an imposing desk each. There was a hand stamp saying 'Office of the Senior Medical Officer', and our office had its own toilet. Now, that really is class. You can sit in state on your own official loo, and contemplate the world. Very posh. Under the hospital we had a large basement pharmacy-cum-storeroom. We had to have enough tablets, medicines, gases, and intravenous fluids to last until the next quarterly supply ship, and to cope with a major disaster should one occur. Such a disaster could perhaps have been the weekly Argentine Air Force passenger plane crash landing, or, more likely, a serious fire affecting a number of wood-built homes. Most were built of wood, and in the frequent high winds a fire could easily have spread from one to another. Therefore we kept a large stock of medical supplies at all times.

These were useful later.

CHAPTER 7

Our patients

FIRST AND FOREMOST, our remit in the Falkland Islands was to provide a complete medical service to the local population, Kelpers, and to expatriates, like ourselves. We were also asked to provide a service to the forty or so Royal Marines of the Naval Party stationed there. They gave us more orthopaedic work (broken bones) than the rest of the population put together. They played rugby football, a 'game', played by men, with funny-shaped balls, where the object is to disable the other side by any means whatsoever. If someone has the ball, then break him. They also picked some remarkably active fights with the more fit, most drunk, Kelpers. We got very competent at fractured jaws and zygomas (cheek bones). In addition we had a weekly radio discussion with the seven doctors posted to bases in Antarctica, working for BAS. It is always good to discuss a difficult case with a colleague. We provided a medical service to passing round-the-world yacht crews, who had usually just come round Cape Horn (that's the way the prevailing winds blow). They would put in to Stanley Harbour to rest, resupply, repair their battered craft, and often to earn a few pounds doing casual labour or providing boat trips around the islands, to pay for their onward journey. This was huge fun for us, as it enabled us to get to the tiny (less than a few square miles) uninhabited islands with our children, on day trips, to see the rarer wild life.

We also provided care for the two huge fishing fleets from Poland and the Soviet Union. The Poles always had one of two huge factory ships moored in the outer harbour, with its own hospital cabin on it. These swapped places every six months to go and sell the catch in the Middle East and Japan. Whilst in the harbour each was served by ten deep-sea trawlers, which brought in their catch to be gutted, packed and frozen, ready for sale. This earned hard currency for the flagging economies of the Soviet block. The Polish ship's doctor, Peter, was a great help to us, as he came to assist when we were working on any of his patients. Sadly, his ship's captain, and the ship's commissar, the political enforcer on the ship, did not trust Peter not to jump ship.

Many of the Polish crew did jump ship, so they were only allowed ashore in very strictly supervised groups. One of these, who had jumped ship and escaped many years previously, and settled permanently on the island, worked for us part-time as an interpreter for our Polish patients. We had no Russian interpreter. We used to go out to the Russian trawlers on a small tender, and jump onto the platform lowered from the ship's side, at the end of either steps or ropes. The tender boat rose and fell four or five feet with each wave, so it was quite scary. Having got to see the patient, we would try to get a history of how the case had started, and what had been done already. This was not easy without a common language. On one occasion Hilary clambered up the ship's side to find a case of late, ruptured appendicitis. The captain was blind drunk on vodka, and could only say 'Oh, Maria, oh Maria' and kept crossing himself. Not exactly a useful history. One of the ship's officers tried various languages with Hilary. He had no English or French at all, and they found common ground in her O level Latin! He was lowered onto the tender on a stretcher, a hazardous descent, and came ashore. We opened him up and washed a load of faeces out of his belly with saline, did an appendicectomy, and cobbled him up again with a plethora of surgical drains. He made an excellent and speedy recovery, so maybe the prayers of the captain to Mary, Mother of Christ, had been heard and answered.

The trouble with the Russians was that they never wanted to take their own sailors back once they had recovered. One more mouth to feed, perhaps, and not the right papers. On one occasion I had actually to refuse to accept a desperately ill patient unless the captain accepted a recovered man in return. He continued to refuse, until I demanded to see the commissar and an interpreter. I explained clearly that I now understood that the mighty Soviet Union was obviously incapable of caring for a working man, a deep sea fisherman, and that it must be an impoverished and powerless nation. The political commissar very quickly overrode the captain's orders, and they took their man.

In the whole of our time in the Falklands the Russians actually gave us the most difficult cases we ever had. A very fit young sailor called Ivan developed appendicitis at sea. Against all advice about appendicitis at sea, which should be treated with antibiotics and rest, the ship's doctor decided to operate at sea. If treated with antibiotics the infection will usually form an appendix mass, which can be removed at leisure in a safe operating environment, by a skilled surgeon. But operate he did using kitchen string for sutures. Needless to say the whole thing broke down, and we ended up with a desperately ill, toxic sailor, with a belly full of putrid muck, a perforated colon, and bits of string floating around in it. I did the only thing I could, under the circumstances, which was to do a simple ileostomy, bringing the small bowel out to the abdominal wall to a bag. Being an incredibly fit young man, Ivan made an excellent recovery, and we sent him back to the Soviet Union in one piece, but with an ileostomy bag. He was with us over Christmas, in the height of summer, and sang 'We Three Kings of Orient Are' in Russian. He, one of the nurses, and I each sang a verse. A great guy, our Ivan.

The Poles were always very grateful for the care we gave them, and kept the hospital and us constantly supplied with twenty-kilogram packs of the very best cod, and 'antar', a fish rather like cod. It made a lovely change from the usual protein, mutton. Sheep outnumbered humans by many hundreds to one on the islands, and were used only for their wool. The only mutton-freezing plant ever tried there, at Ajax Bay, failed for lack of a profitable market (the buildings were used later) so mutton was available in excess, and was sold ready-butchered at sixteen or seventeen pence a quarter, or under a pound for a whole carcase. The farmers would give their chickens a whole, cleaned carcase every few weeks as a protein-rich diet.

CHAPTER 8

The job

THE LOCAL POPULATION consisted of 1,700 people. One thousand lived in the Capital Cathedral Village of Stanley. The basic structures of civilisation were there in Stanley – Government House, the Government Secretariat, primary and secondary schools, the hospital, cathedral, HM Customs and harbourmaster (all one man), and a shop selling almost everything except fresh foods. And three good pubs. Drinking is taken very seriously in the islands.

Our house was about a mile from the main town, and the sea plane shed and ramp (Stanley Marine Airport) was a further mile along the inner harbour wall on the other side of us. A further two miles along, at the end of the inner harbour, was Moody Brook, the barracks of the Royal Marines. The land airport, Stanley International Airport, was about four miles the other way, via Stanley, on a little peninsula of land. So the thousand lucky inhabitants of Stanley had it all. The other seven hundred lived in about thirty settlements, varying in size from a hundred to two souls apiece, spread all over the islands. There are two main islands, East Falkland, where Stanley lies on the north-east coast, and West Falkland, where Fox Bay is the largest settlement, then with a population of nearly a hundred people. Beyond the main islands are about three hundred smaller, but quite substantial islands. Sheep alone inhabited most of these, and they were just visited from time to time for shearing, sheep care, sex, and things like that.

We held daily clinics in the hospital, just like ordinary English general practice clinics. The nurses ran their own ante-natal clinics as well. The only difference from English practice was that any blood tests, X-rays, or bacteriology examinations were done then and there in the hospital. This actually makes general practice work more exciting for the doctor, as the decisions about what to look for, and what to look at, are entirely up to you. If you want to do complicated and time-consuming tests then that is fine. Get on and do them. Yourself. Certainly we did, with much help from our laboratory technician-radiographer (trained by the British Council, God bless them, and very many thanks). There were no pompous pathologists or radiologists to ask if the tests were really necessary. So the Stanley patients were easy to reach and care for. But what about the seven hundred or so in 'the Camp'? The Camp is anywhere outside Stanley. The Camp population had previously been visited as and when necessary only. My predecessor had not been fond of flying. He was said to have disliked it even more than women doctors. He may occasionally have had a drink before going up. Rumours, rumours. He certainly tried to stop one of our excellent pilots from flying on the grounds that he was intellectually unsuited to the task – an odd charge. Hilary, who had taken charge of health care in all the forest settlements in Swaziland, would have none of this. She drew up a huge wall chart in my office, with each of the thirty Camp settlements on it, along with the population of each, marked against an ongoing diary. The smallest settlements were marked with twelve-weekly visits, the largest with two-weekly, and the others pro rata. This rota meant that ante-natal care, smear tests, childhood immunisations, post-natal care, along with chronic disease management like high blood pressure, diabetes, epilepsy, thyroid disease, etc., could be cared for in a regular, planned way. This suited most of the solid, hard-working Camp people very well indeed. The only losers were those who had previously had their shopping trips into Stanley paid for by Government, as medical expenses. Curbing this freed up money for use in real medical care.

The travel was fantastic. Each doctor had the regular use of one aeroplane for one day a week. The plane had many other duties. The highest priority was, quite rightly, not routine medicine, but the post. When there was post for a settlement it had to be delivered within a set time. Standards, you know. It was usually delivered by drop. The plane flew low over the settlement, flaps fully down, throttled back, as if about to land. The person sitting next to the pilot had to open his or her window, hold out a weighted bag against the fierce slip wind, and wait for the command 'Go' from the pilot. At this moment the passenger, often the doctor, had to hurl the bag down, very hard indeed, so that it did not get caught up in the back of the aircraft, where the slipstream tried to take it. The pilots and farmers marked us out of ten for whether we were accurate in our dropping technique or not. They never taught us that at medical school.

We had three aeroplanes. Two were Beaver float planes. Each had two canoe-shaped floats almost the length of the aircraft. They had

A patient rowing me back to the Beaver float plane.

the old Merlin rotary engines, about sixteen cylinders arranged round the central propeller shaft like a huge clock face. These beautiful, noisy craft took pilot and one passenger in the front, and three side by side in the back. Alternatively, the three back seats could be taken out and replaced by a stretcher. A problem with the Beavers was that they needed about four feet of water depth to float in safely. Not all settlements had a suitable jetty, and the tides were often very high, so most jetties could only be used at certain tides. Many flights had, therefore, to be met by rowing boat. Great if you are fit and agile, but nasty if you are on a stretcher with a broken leg. The Kelpers were expert at handling stretchers, and pigs, on and off the rowing boats and the plane's floats. More than once I feared a good ducking getting from the tossing rowing boat onto the float of the plane. The Kelpers would then pass the patient, on a stretcher, with amazing ease onto the float, then on up into the back of the plane. A combination of strength, sea skill and experience, I suppose.

Our third aeroplane, rather conventionally, landed on land. It was a twin-engined Brittan Norman Islander, much used in the Scottish Highlands and Islands. Again, it had two front seats, then four pairs of two behind, which could be replaced with a purpose-designed stretcher-bed, with an integral seat for the doctor. It was a brilliant plane for a doctor with a sick or injured patient, but more of that later.

CHAPTER 9

FIGAS

THE FALKLAND ISLANDS Government Air Service (FIGAS) were an interesting lot. The Director was a Kelper with civil service experience. He knew every detail of every settlement's beaches, bays and landing strip. Not a pilot himself, he knew a great deal about flying, and the decision on whether there would be any flying at all on any particular day was his. He knew the fogs, winds and sea conditions better than most. He was a sturdily built redhead called Gerald Cheek and was a credit to the islands. The pilots, of course, always had the final say as to whether to take off or not, but some would have risked flying in difficult circumstances just for the challenge.

The little Beaver float plane struggled in fog, high winds and rough seas. We could usually manage in winds of up to forty knots as long as the sea was not too rough. The Islander could cope with slightly higher winds as long as they were in the direction of the landing strip. It is very difficult to land an aircraft in a strong side wind, and we had gale force winds on average one day in four. When there was, exceptionally, no wind at all then fog tended to develop. On one memorable occasion I was coming back to Stanley with a woman in labour. (They were meant to come into Stanley a month before they were due, but this lady had cut it a bit fine. So Mike Selwood, the pilot, and I had gone out to get her in the Islander.) On our return we found a sixty-knot wind at right angles to the runway. Mike was delighted. He was a very experienced commercial pilot. He simply landed us very slowly, very neatly, across the width of the runway, and taxied straight to the ambulance waiting in the lee of the airport building. She had a healthy baby boy.

The Beaver float planes were old. An RAF sergeant mechanic maintained them, and did so very well. But they did give trouble from time to time. The mechanical fuel pumps were none too reliable, and the front seat passenger had to be good at using the emergency hand pump to keep the engine going if the automatic pump failed. They also had very dodgy back door catches. Hilary's door flew open in the middle of one flight home when she was sitting next to the door. Seat belt on, of course, but still a bit unnerving. So the Government Chief plumber, Tom, who was sitting in the middle seat next to her, put an arm reassuringly around her, and held on. Hilary was very grateful for this. But on landing in the harbour, immediately outside both his and our houses, he suddenly let go. As was her custom, his wife was watching the plane landing through her binoculars. He did not want to have to explain his arm being around Hilary. Rolling pins, and all that.

I was aware, however, of a terribly sad flying event. One of the doctors before us (not the woman-hating one mentioned earlier) was an amateur pilot. Flying with the professional pilot, he had the controls. The plane crashed into the sea. The professional pilot died of a heart attack. I later found that careful checks had been made on Hilary and myself to ensure that we were not amateur pilots.

One person I did not like on the Islands was the Governor. I found him a pompous man. (It takes one to spot one.) He had been a Battle of Britain pilot but he was a little man in more ways than one. One of my nurses had fallen in love with a Kelper in one of the smaller settlements. The love was not initially requited. She went to stay with him for a few days but things got no better. She took an overdose and he found her deeply unconscious, and radioed for help. Mike and I went at once. It was a difficult, dusk landing, and we bundled her unconscious body onto a stretcher and into the Beaver (probably her most dangerous moment). We got her to the hospital, pumped her out, and maintained her safely on a ventilator until she recovered some time later. When I reported the incident to the Governor, with some pride in both the hospital staff's and the pilot's professionalism, the little man's response was 'What a pity she didn't die. It would have been a lot easier to replace her than all the reporting that must now ensue.'

When my children first met him he was wearing a dark blue tie with large gold-coloured dots on it. They christened him 'the man with the golden balls'. It stuck.

I recall a much happier flying incident. A common form of cross country travel is by motorbike. They go well over grass and heather, but are dodgy over stream beds. Young men traditionally go to a neighbouring settlement, perhaps twenty miles away, on pay day for a booze up. This is fine, but crossing the stream beds is quite dangerous if sober, and can be quite catastrophic if drunk. I got quite good at picking bits of skull out of brains. It is quite incredible how much brain tissue you can manage without, especially if you are young. Well, there was a nasty one. The farmer found him two days later, in the rocks by the stream, with his skull smashed well in. He was still breathing. The farmer gave a very good description of the situation over the radio. Captain Mike, as the children called him, and I studied the map. There was no prepared airstrip for the Islander anywhere near, and the nearest safe sea landing for a Beaver was four miles away from him, over very rough terrain. He would certainly be well dead after that ride. Mike recalled a flattish paddock near the offending stream. His wife, a skilled air stewardess, joined us. We stripped the eight back seats out of the Islander, fixed in the purpose built stretcher and attendant's seat, complete with oxygen and intravenous fluid sets, and took off. The paddock was as Mike had recalled it. He made a perfect landing, and we lifted the young man very carefully onto the stretcher. He really was in a bad way, with severe hypothermia as well as a gaping head injury. He was carried gently to the plane by other Kelpers, who really thought his last hour had come. We made a smooth take off, and an hour later he was in the operating theatre. No anaesthetic needed as we picked the pebbles, headlight glass and bits of skull out of his brain, stopped the bleeding, gave him a couple of pints (blood – he had had enough beer) and he woke up two weeks later. His mother swore he was brighter after the accident than before.

CHAPTER 10

The gang of four

FOUR OF US made a rather unholy alliance – Mike Selwood, the pilot, Dick Baker, our neighbour, the Chief Secretary and Deputy Governor, Garry Noott and me. Dick balanced the Governor perfectly. Just as the one was small both in stature and in mind, so the other was large in both. Dick Baker was also a jovial man with a keen sense of responsibility, and a lovely sense of humour. We discussed all our really difficult decisions with him, like whether to operate on a patient myself, or whether to send them back to England for surgery, and he never once failed to listen carefully, and then respond with a well-measured answer. He suggested the 'one for one' swaps of Russian seamen and worked out how to go about sorting out a case of child abuse. He sussed out my apprehension about the Argentine people, and said 'I think you regard them as Dagos, don't you Daniel?' He was later appointed Governor of Saint Helena.

The fourth villain of the piece was Major Garry Noott, or the Newt, as he was affectionately known. He commanded the Naval Party of Royal Marines, about forty of them. He had one officer, a second lieutenant, who was useful to us. Because any technical information about the Russian fleet of deep-sea trawlers was potentially useful to the Royal Navy during the cold war, we trained him as a medical assistant. He carried my bags, held the patient's arm correctly for me to take blood, and could record blood pressure, pulse, temperature and respiration. He would come as my 'assistant' whenever I was called to a Russian vessel. They tell me he gained some useful information. He was said to be a good pistol shot. I love target shooting. After some Marines had broken a few more bones playing football, and I had cobbled them up a bit, as usual, he was detailed off to thank me, and ask if there was anything the Marines could do for me. I asked if he could give me a good go with my favourite weapon, the nine-millimetre Browning automatic pistol. He readily agreed, and set up a number of practice targets. We both did our best. A sergeant stood behind us to see fair play. I won outright.

Shock. Horror. Can't let the men know a damned doctor is a better shot than their own Royal Marine officer.

So, there were the four of us. Dick Baker had the brains, I was the doctor, Mike was the pilot and Garry was the Royal Marine with access to duty-free gin. We sort of worked together. I think it was initially the Newt's fault. He invited the rest of us, and Hilary, to be honorary members of his Officers' Mess. After all, it's a bit lonely to have an Officers' Mess with only two members. Especially when the other member is courting the Governor's daughter. It was time-consuming. They married, which was good for his career. I just hope they are happily married now, but I don't know.

Now, relationships exist at various levels. Sex is probably one of the most basic. The Royal Marines had a beautiful female cat, the darling of them all, called Suzy Wong. We had a healthy, complete, real male cat. The two- or three-mile walk along the harbourside road to Moody Brook, where Suzy Wong lived, was a pleasant stroll for our cat, Mandla (SiSwati for 'the strong one'). The Marines, never slow to come forward, loved this beautiful relationship, and always made sure that Mandla came home safely. Very proper. The Royal Marines also kept geese, as we did. At the end of each mating season we had to have a reallocation of each of our flocks, because geese also form strong personal relationships. Down one from sex perhaps comes food. Procreation first, then consolidation. Well, Royal Marine cooking, although adequate, does leave just a little to be desired. I had got the vegetable garden and the hothouse, both producing bounte-ously. We had chickens, ducks and geese. Dick Baker, in his high office, had the occasional treat, like a joint of pork. Mike, the pilot, could be bribed with a cut of beef to fly an ill-tempered boar from one settlement to another for necessary reproductive purposes. Hilary was a first-rate cook. So it just worked out. Garry's wife was in England, as was Mike's most of the time. Hilary, and Dick Baker's wife, Connie, both knew the way to a man's heart is through his stomach. So every week or so we would all meet up for a superb meal, with plenty of duty free, and discuss the previous week's events, and put the world to rights. Very often our three children, and the Bakers' two daughters, were with us until bedtime.

The five children learned to keep a quiet, low profile during these dinners, and as a result were allowed to stay up later than usual, listening to the affairs of government, medicine, aviation and the military – a rare and privileged education that has had a profound effect on our three, at least. On one occasion the four men, two women, and five children were all together at table. It was at Dick Baker's house. A radio message came in that there had been a terrible accident at a settlement. It was late into the evening. Mike and I had already had a drink or two. Out came the maps. Mike wanted to land the Islander in the dark, using crossed Land-Rover headlamps as markers for the airstrip. Dick and Garry looked worried, as did the ladies. Dick got the farm manager on the radio. The man had been making a new fence. He had put a large post in the ground, and pulled five strands of barbed wire tight away from it with a tractor pulling the next stake. The first post came loose. Pulled by the five stretched strands of wire, it came at him like a rocket, and crushed his head, taking half away with it. From the description Dick was sure he was dead. The farm manager agreed, but the young wife wanted death confirmed by a doctor. So Hilary got to speak to him on the radio. She asked the manager bluntly whether the patient was alive or not. The reply was 'Well, if he was a sheep, then no. He is very definitely dead.' So Dick Baker told Mike and me to shut up, and go home to bed. We set off at dawn next morning to see him. He was indeed very, very dead.

CHAPTER 11

The Black List

W E HAD A wonderful institution in the Falkland Islands called the
Black List. Because of the very serious problems of both
chronic and acute alcoholism a system was devised whereby anyone
who was endangering either themselves or other people through
drink could be put on the list for up to a year. It would then be a
serious, punishable offence for them to buy, possess, or to have drunk
any alcohol at all, and for anyone to give, sell or procure it to or for
them. The names on the current list would be displayed on the town
hall and the police station notice boards. Punishment for infringement
of the Black List order would be a hefty fine, or imprisonment.

An example. The local hotel had an Argentine cook. She lived in
a caravan behind the hotel and she had a man in the caravan for
company. He drank. Hilary was first on call that night. The phone
went at 3 a.m. He was dead in bed, and his lady friend was ululating
in grief, waking everyone for a great distance around. Her beloved
man was dead. Hilary got up to examine the corpse. He was vastly
tall. And fat. He was indeed dead. Dead drunk. Actually he was
dangerously drunk, deeply unconscious, and in grave danger of
vomiting and choking to death on it. This is the most common cause
of death from acute alcohol poisoning. Hepatitis is from chronic,
ongoing alcoholism. Hilary could not leave him there in the little
caravan. The hotel staff said there was no way they could move his
vast bulk up to the hospital. By this time Hilary was on a short fuse.
She told them they most certainly would move him there, even if it
meant taking their damned caravan as well, with him in it. They did
move him, much as one moves a sick cow. The hospital nurses were
none too pleased at being woken to receive him at 4 a.m., and gave
him a rough few days of it.

We actually had a padded room with window bars and a reinforced
door in the hospital for these customers, so that we could cope with
the ensuing state of delirium tremens in relative safety. When they
had the d.t.s badly they could be quite violent and dangerous, both
to themselves and to their carers. They needed a lot of care to stop

them dying of heat exhaustion and electrolyte imbalance. We would call in a policeman or two to hold them steady whilst I gave them a huge injection of chlorpromazine. When they were safely asleep, we would set up an intravenous drip to rehydrate them, and get a forced diuresis (pouring fluid into a vein so that it passed out again via the kidneys as urine, plus alcohol). We got very skilled at this, with plenty of practice and never lost one.

Anyway, this cook's beloved recovered, and wanted to go back to her caravan to start all over again. A quick call was made to Toddy, the Chief of Police and Immigration, and to Mr Bennett, the magistrate, and it was off to court with one badly hung-over client. In court the magistrate came in and the constable told everyone present to stand up. He heaved the patient onto his feet.

'Yes, Doctor, tell me what happened.'

The scene was set.

'Yes,' said Mr Bennett, 'a clear case for the List. How long would you recommend, Doctor?'

'One year, sir.'

(To our hero.) 'The doctor says one year. You caused an awful lot of trouble at the hospital. What have you got to say for yourself?'

'Three months maximum, sir. I never hit anyone.'

Pause for deliberation.

'Six months.'

Papers signed, notice posted.

'Stand up.'

The magistrate left the court.

Very formal, very proper.

One of my regulars on the Black List had to be kept on it virtually all the time. He was the Government Chief Ratcatcher, on the payroll of my hospital. Rats had come onto the islands aboard the old sailing ships. They thrived on our wonderful refuse disposal system — a huge, stinking pile of rotting garbage downwind of Stanley, with old food aplenty on it. Anyone who kept chickens or pigs, or flour for bread-making, was plagued by them. So you sent for Gooks, Rat Catcher by Appointment. He really was a lovely character, with countless tales to tell of rats of fame and promise. I spent hours with him, listening at the ratmaster's feet. He wore an enormous blackened brown raincoat, with huge pockets filled with poisons of every sort in little brown bags. He would shuffle off, leaving small deposits of poison here and there. Rather MacBeth-witches-like. (We named our next cat after him.) But he drank. As he had already been severely damaged by alcohol, even a little was very dangerous. So each day that he came off the List I took him along to Mr Bennett for a year's renewal. No policeman was necessary. It was all very gentlemanly. But imagine the scene in the very formal court with me, a bit embarrassed at bringing in my friend, and Gooks, in his amazing coat, the poisons bulging from his pockets. He never walked. He always shuffled, sideways, in a crab-like manner, eyes darting all over the place for any sign of a rat.

Another regular was a highly skilled Kelper sheepshearer. Many came for a few weeks from Australia and New Zealand in the shearing season. It was highly paid, skilled work. One was reputed always to travel by first-class air passage. Well, this Kelper shearer was always paid in full, in cash, at the end of each shearing season. It was a lot of money. All his creditors from the previous year would stand in line to regain their loans and debts. Then the fun began. He would drink himself to oblivion, then he'd be into hospital, pumped out and off to see Mr Bennett. He was one of Hilary's special patients.

The policeman, Hilary and the shearer would be in court.

'One year, please.'

'Three months, please.'

The policeman would intervene:

'He was very violent, Sir. He socked me one.'

'One year it is then.'

'All stand up.'

The magistrate would go out. The shearer would turn to Hilary. 'I don't care about that. I'm going to Comodoro, where I can drink as much as I like, and you can't stop me, Love.'

Big grin.

He was quite right. The Argentines, along with some of their other undesirable characteristics at that time, suffered from a horrible disease called hyperinflation. Their peso, or peeso, as we called it, was of ever falling value, and no one wanted it. A Falkland Island pound, with the Financial Secretary's signature on it, was real money. So they would accept him happily each year, take enough money off him for his return fare home, sell him enough booze to keep him subdued, and let him drink until he was broke. Then he would be bundled onto the next plane back and would reach home dead broke. He would be safe until the end of the next shearing season when it would start again.

The Financial Secretary tells of when he himself had a little too much in Comodoro. He ran out of ready cash and an Argentine declined his cheque. He wrote out, then and there, a perfectly legal, if individual, Falkland Island banknote, and signed it. He told the waiter to take it to the hotel manager, and compare the signature with a standard banknote. A red-faced manager returned, muttering apologies.

The Financial Secretary was a practical man, and in winter he loved to toboggan down the steep main road leading down, through Stanley, to the harbour main jetty. He always managed to stop just in time, which is where the skill came in. This activity was always accompanied by a substantial amount of alcohol 'to keep the chill winds away.' A rotund friend did not have the Financial Secretary's head for alcohol, and fell gently into the snow, drunk as could be. He was totally unable to stand up on the ice, and his home was at the top of the hill, so our senior government officer tied this incapable body onto the sledge, attached it to the back of his Land-Rover, and towed him safely home.

His wife was not amused.

CHAPTER 12

The cloistered life

THE CATHEDRAL was a building, a church, and an institution. It was a huge, redbrick, classical Victorian church-style building. It had oil-fired heating, and a mouldering church smell quite of its own – very holy. The bricks had been fired in England and imported by steamship. It was the biggest, most imposing building in Stanley, only to be challenged by Fort Louise at Port Louise, where the French had their capital when they violently and illegally seized the islands 200 years ago. Very French. Even Government House could not match the cathedral. I always wondered what Golden Balls thought of God having a bigger residence than himself. On the approach to the cathedral was a huge arch constructed from four whale jawbones. Whales were occasionally seen around the Falklands, but porpoise, seal, elephant seal and sea lions were far more common and easy to see. They would come ashore in the breeding season, and appeared quite unafraid of humans, so we could walk among them. In front of the cathedral on the harbour wall was one of the three original masts of the first effective British steam ship, the SS *Great Britain*. She, like so many other great and famous sea-going vessels, had come around Cape Horn in a storm, and the insurance loss adjustors had written her off as being beyond economical repair. So for half a century she lay grounded and rotting in the harbour, being used as a wool storehouse. Eventually the Marine Conservation Society realised her unique historical value. She is now a prize museum ship, back in Britain. Maybe they will reclaim the mast too, one day.

Within the cathedral were high altar, choir stalls, a fine carved wooden screen (you have to separate clergy and choir from hoi polloi), and serried rank upon rank of pews. The pulpit was to the front of, and the font to the rear of, the common people. You preach at them from the front, and let them in at the back should they want a baptism. The choir consisted of two powerful (in all ways) middle-aged ladies, the wife of an Argentine teacher, and Fred. Well, Fred. He made a dreadful noise. The story was that his mother had run a stake down his throat as a baby, to try to improve his voice. It

42

didn't work. Don't try it. Please. He 'sang' so loud after that, to avoid her repeating the process, that the community decided the only safe place for him was in the cathedral choir. You got used to it after a time. A long time. The Argentine himself was a problem. A big problem. The tradition was that if the Governor was at evensong then, at the end of the service, we would all stand up and sing the first and last verses of the National Anthem We only sang the middle verse on special occasions. Well, this miserable Argentine would not stand up for the occasion. He persistently sat, po-faced, throughout our patriotic performance. He did once stand up when I managed to stand in front of him, on his toes. But he tended to avoid me after that.

In case you don't know the middle verse, which you ought to, here it is.

O Lord our God, arise,
Scatter our enemies,
And make them fall.
Confound their politics,
Frustrate their knavish tricks,
On thee our hopes we fix,
God save us all.

I believe it was written with the French in mind.

The Falkland Islands Radio Service broadcast the service, long wave, every third week. The Roman Catholics had one week in three, and all the rest, Wesleyan Methodists, Baha'i, etc, shared the final three-weekly slot. Being a deacon of the Church of England, I often preached. When old Harry, the chaplain, was away in camp or on leave, I took the lot. It was not until some years later that I learned that our services, the only proper Anglican services south of Belize, Central America, could be heard over much of Chile, Bolivia and the Argentine. I hope my sermons weren't too bad, boring or heretical.

The other respectable church on the islands was the Roman Catholic Church. They had a monsignor, roughly equivalent to one of our senior bishops, and a priest. The priest was a gem, Irish to the core, and very hard-working. He was always there when we wanted him in the hospital. The Polish deep-sea trawler men were Roman Catholic to a man, despite the official Soviet position. The priest would do anything to help us to help them, like driving up to the marines at Moody Brook at 4 a.m. to get volunteers to give blood for an emergency operation. The marines loved him too. He would visit them on exercise, pockets full of chocolates and the odd nip of brandy. Our own Church of England chaplain was a pacifist, and did not approve of marines and things. Monsignor Spraggon, a personal friend of His Holiness the Pope, supported Father Moynihan in every way he could. He features much later in this little story. They both welcomed me into their church at mass.

When Old Harry was away and there was a funeral to be taken, it was taken by me. As Senior Medical Officer, I had to sign a rather official-looking letter releasing the body for burial, saying that the body had died a natural death, and no further examination or investigation was indicated. The officiating chaplain at the funeral had to sign a book, held in the cathedral, to say that he had received this letter. So I had the great pleasure on several occasions of writing this very pompous letter to myself.

CHAPTER 13

HMS *Endurance*

I CAME TO KNOW the inside of the police station rather too well. As well as lengthy discussions with the inspector-cum-immigration officer, Toddy, about everything under the sun, we had a prisoner. In a fit of pique he had slit his wife's throat, and then his own. His wife died, but he was resuscitated, to his great regret, by my predecessor. A high court judge and defence and prosecution lawyers were shipped out from England, and he had been sentenced to life imprisonment. It was decided by the judicial authorities in England that he must serve the term in a British jail, with proper facilities for 'life' prisoners. He had a pleasant little flat prepared for him at the back of the police station, until passage to England could be found for him. The difficulty was finding a passage. The Argentine authorities flatly refused to let him go on one of their planes. They had a stranglehold on air travel, because they ran the only flight, in a military transport plane, between the Falklands and Buenos Aires. The captain of HMS *Endurance*, the British Antarctic patrol vessel, was asked to take him back to Britain, on the grounds that there was a safe little prison cell aboard the vessel, for miscreant sailors. He refused, on the grounds that having a murderer aboard might upset the crew. (The man should be court martialled for cowardice in the face of a problem, in my opinion.) After about six months a passage was found for him aboard the British Antarctic Survey (BAS) ship *Bransfield*. At least they had the spine to face the challenge. In fact, when sober, he was a charming, quiet, rather slow man, and no threat to anyone. We visited him regularly in his little prison, and got to know and like him. We also visited Kelpers in the cells when they had been drunk and fighting. When they picked fights with the marines, the Kelpers always came off worse, but they could also do a good deal of damage to each other. It all made work for the working man, and policeman, to do.

Visits of HMS *Endurance* were a nightmare for the doctors. It was rumoured that for a very long time condoms were not issued to any sailor coming ashore on the Falkland Islands. This was to improve the

45

very restricted local gene pool. True or not, they certainly were not used. Abortion for social purposes was illegal on the islands, and I did not do any. A few interesting looking babies arrived. But that was not the major problem, which was the 'Montevideo Special.' Montevideo, where the ship called in for 'recreational visits', had a few ladies of ill repute. They had serviced more men than was good for them. They had done more naughty things than they should have done. Big bugs have little bugs upon their back to bite them. Little bugs have littler bugs, and so on ad infinitum. Montevideo gonorrhoea must be one of the most potent, multiantibiotic-resistant bugs in the world. We never could cure it, and these hairy sailors kept offering it around like smarties to our pure virgins. One unfortunate Marine came to us with a 'dose', after some shore leave in Monte. Hopefully, very hopefully, we ordered ten large doses of multiple antibiotics, along with an excretion-blocking drug probenecid, also used in the treatment of gout, to be given by daily injection deep into the muscle of the buttock. Very painful indeed. The puritanical nurse thrusting the last of these deep injections into his bared backside said, 'There. That will teach you not to do it again!' She was dumbstruck, for the first and last time ever, when he replied, 'No, Ma'am. It was well worth it!'

Hilary and I were so concerned by the ravages of the Montevideo Special that I decided to go and see the captain commanding Her Majesty's Ship, who could not take a reformed murderer back to Britain for us. He chose not to meet me, but referred me instead to the first officer, his sort of sidekick, and to the ship's medical officer. The poor medical officer was polite and pleasant enough. He knew the problem only too well, but was powerless to do anything about it because the captain wouldn't let him. The first officer was a different matter altogether. Who the hell did I think I was, wasting his time, and contaminating his warship of the Royal Navy? If his sailors wanted a dose of Montevideo Special, then that was up to them, not me! Bloody medics, always wanting an easy life. What did we think we were paid for? I gave up. The trouble is, if a man gets it, he gets a profuse urethral discharge (a thick drip from the prick), feels that he is peeing razor blades, and stains his underpants, a sure give-away. He tends to seek help. When a lady gets it she may just think she has a urinary infection, but she can very soon become infertile when it infects her fallopian tubes. Not fair, really.

The next dripping visit of HMS *Endurance* was no happier. The sailors played the Royal Marines at rugby. Now, if organised sport is the root of all evil in mankind, which it probably is, then rugby is surely the essence of the devil incarnate. They set out to hurt each other, and did so. Two smashed knees, one ruined back, and a fractured femur. And they didn't even take their refuse back with them. 'We only have fit men on our ships.' Later, all too shortly later, we were to discover that the Royal Navy has real warships, with real naval officers aboard, men aboard prepared to fight for their country, and to lay down their lives for us.

The *Endurance* did get one thing right, though. They took his Excellency the Governor on a visit to Antarctica, the British regions of which he was also governor. They took him on a visit to one of the bases in one of their two Lynx helicopters, and actually crashed it. The other one rescued him unscathed. Another place, another time, perhaps . . .?

CHAPTER 14

Camp life

OUR MEDICAL VISITS to the Camp settlements were varied and interesting. I came to admire the resilience, ingenuity and fortitude of those living in tiny communities, often as small as two or three people, in very remote areas. Often the three-monthly medical visit, also bringing them their mail and supplies from Stanley, would be the only visit they had had that quarter. The pilot was always made very welcome, and if he was staying during the medical visit he would be well fed too. Often, though, the visiting doctor would be left by the plane whilst other, local, journeys were made. This would leave an hour or two after any medical work to explore the locality.

All settlements had elaborate arrangements for sorting sheep, shearing them, and for wool sorting. Each had a store, with basic foods enough for a few months, in case of difficulties with resupply. Heavy goods like rice, flour, sugar and beer were delivered by sea. Every household in the Camp took great pride in the bread they baked. The arrangements for slaughtering and sharing out a cow or a pig were basic, but well practised over the years. Many took great pride in horse-riding, and there were annual 'races' in Stanley.

On the downside was the rubbish. The best farmers dug huge pits, burnt down any household rubbish to prevent fly breeding, and eventually covered the rubbish-filled pits with a deep layer of soil. Some farmers, sadly, just dumped their rubbish on a convenient beach, causing a foul-smelling eyesore. Every household, both in Stanley and in the Camp, had its own designated peat pit. Cubes of peat were cut with a very sharp ten-inch spade, and piled, or 'rickled', to dry. When dry, usually toward the end of summer, it could be stored under cover, and used to heat both homes and water. A block of wet peat weighs around ten kilograms, so peat digging is very heavy work.

Travel around the Camp was a challenge. There were no roads outside Stanley itself. Air travel by Beaver or Islander has been described. Sea travel was well organised for cargo, but could be used by passengers occasionally. It was mainly for the delivery of bulk

48

goods and stores to the settlements, and to bring wool, the only commercial product of the islands, to Stanley for export. There was a sturdy little vessel, called the MV *Forrest*, that motored around the islands on a regular basis. It was not a comfortable, or fast, form of travel for humans. Most travel was done overland. Traditionally, horses were the best way to get around. They did not sink easily into the peat bogs, and you could do a comfortable four miles an hour on horseback. Many of the horses were of a rather wild and free spirit, and riding could be a bit of a challenge. It was safer for a novice to go by foot, at about two and a half miles an hour. In the long summers it was a real pleasure to walk from one settlement to another. One could walk for several days without meeting another human being. But neither horse nor feet are good for carrying heavy loads very far. A Land-Rover was best for this, or a tractor and trailer.

Because of the plentiful peat bogs most Land-Rover journeys across country involved a few boggings. You get used to them. We all carried bump jacks, planks, shovels and matting in order to de-bog. Some vehicles were fitted with winches. When bogged, you dug a deep hole somewhere in the right direction, and buried your spare wheel in it as an anchor. Then you tried to winch the vehicle out if its bog hole, using the towrope. It sometimes worked. Due to boggings it was reasonable to estimate journey times at about two and a half miles an hour on average when going across country. It was challenging work.

There were no primary schools in any but the largest of the Camp settlements, so peripatetic Camp teachers were appointed. They would stay a few days in each household with primary school-age children in it, and teach them and their parents enough to carry on until the next visit. The visiting doctor would often share a plane with these teachers, and very interesting company they made too. So a sheep farmer's wife was expected to be cook, baker, dairymaid and keeper of the fowl, to keep the boiler going, make the butter, and be a schoolteacher as well. The women tended to be brighter than the men. They drank less, worked long hours, and had to keep up their own education at least to primary school level. All secondary school-age children had to board, or live with friends or family in Stanley, where the only secondary school was situated. The men in Camp were very, very strong from cutting and rickling peat, sorting sheep by heaving them over fences into pens, building fences and carrying huge crates of beer. Sadly, many of the men eventually developed quite severe osteoarthritis (worn-out joints) of the knees, hips and shoulders relatively young, and had to retire early.

Another frequent traveller to Camp was the Government vet. Hydatid disease was common in the islands. This is a nasty disease passed between dogs, dog urine on grass, contaminated grass to sheep, big cysts in the sheep, then back to dogs when they eat the infested sheep, or their offal. Sheepdogs are essential to sheep care. The big problem is that humans can contract the disease, usually from their dogs. The life cycle of the disease is not completed in man, but it causes large, often multiple, cysts in a person's lung, liver or brain. As this can cause long-term, severe disability, including epilepsy, the vet put a great deal of effort into trying to persuade farmers not to let their dogs eat sheep offal, to keep good standards of hygiene among their valuable sheepdogs, and in inspecting meat to monitor the disease. The doctors had to be adept at diagnosing the disease at an early stage before severe damage was done, and controlling, but very seldom curing, the disease with drugs. When the vet was on leave the doctors had to stand in for him as best we could. That is usually easy enough. It's a bit like paediatrics. Small children can't tell you exactly what is wrong with them; they just look unwell, or vomit, cough, or do some other unsociable action. And so it is with animals. You just have to observe, listen to, and feel them. The main difference between child and animal medical practice is that the children tend to bite less. (Watch out, though. When children do bite, it can be nasty.) Our worst veterinary problem on the islands was a large, valuable, much loved sheepdog with a cauliflower ear. The ear was bleeding internally, into the flap of the ear, and the dog was distraught with pain and irritation. We had to operate. I weighed the dog, and gave him the same dose of an injected anaesthetic that I would give a man of that weight. It did nothing but annoy the dog even more, and he turned round and bit me. I doubled the dose. Same effect. I doubled the dose again. Still no useful effect. I gave up. He had now had seven times a suitable dose for his weight. I then made a dog-shaped face-mask from a metal coat hanger and gauze, and dripped a very old-fashioned anaesthetic liquid, chloroform, onto it. It worked a treat. The operation was fine, but, like humans anaesthetised with chloroform, the dog vomited a good deal during the recovery period. Messy.

CHAPTER 15

Gardening

GARDENING IN Stanley was a joy to me. We had nearly two acres, on a gently north-facing slope, sloping down toward the inner harbour. Remember everything is back to front there, in the Southern Hemisphere, where the world is upside down. So north-facing there is facing the sun all day, like south-facing in Britain. The main kitchen garden, about a third of an acre, had been well-worked in the past. After borrowing a petrol engine-driven Rotavator for a weekend, and digging the land over, I used our beloved long-wheelbase Land-Rover to make several trips to the beach to bring home huge loads of washed-up, rotting, stinking kelp. It smells like an unwashed cowshed, or a urinal on a hot day and it makes a magnificent compost and fertiliser. It was the only time that our wonderful, downwind, neighbours, the Bakers, complained. They didn't actually complain as such; they just put on a handkerchief face-mask as they passed by.

Between rows of kelp, about eighteen inches high, I planted beetroot, turnip, parsnip, cabbage, kale, leaf beet, cauliflower, sprouts and lettuce. The lettuce failed but everything else grew enough for our family of five, our magnificent dinner parties, and more. We learnt to keep the cabbage growing all the year round by growing about eight varieties, and picking a single leaf from each of the most vigorous plants at any time of the year. Twenty leaves add up to a fair helping of greens for everyone, and left all the plants still growing vigorously, even in midwinter. Fresh greens were a welcome addition to the plentiful mutton, and the only greens available in the West Store, the main shop in Stanley, were desiccated cabbage, which made a tasteless, fibrous green slush on being rehydrated and cooked and was not a favourite with the children. The store also sold desiccated mixed vegetables, cut into little cubes, which were just edible in a stew, but not recommended by themselves.

Until we got the garden up and running these dull, dried vegetables were all we could buy. I hesitated to accept gifts from the hospital garden, as these were really meant for the patients and living-in staff, and there was not much to spare. Our previous post had been in

Swaziland, where fruit and vegetables were cheap and plentiful, and of very high quality. I well remember our joy when a beautiful red-haired woman gave us a gift of some fresh turnip tops to use as fresh greens. They tasted delicious after a few weeks of desiccated desecration of good vegetables. I later delivered her first baby. We laughed about those turnip tops.

Did you know that you can eat the green, growing leafy tops of most root vegetables? Beetroot, turnip, swede, radish. They are all excellent if you are short of greens. But avoid potato and carrot leaves which are no good at all, cooked or raw. The former is a little poisonous, the latter an unpredictable laxative. As well as our productive kitchen garden, we had a small fruit garden, with currants and gooseberries – not much of a crop for the space and effort, but a pleasant taste change all the same, and good for jams and pies.

The essential for Falkland gardening is a good windbreak. This might consist of a line of gorse bushes upwind of your plot, and then a line of casuarina pine, up to about twelve feet high, and then a fence. The fence must be of intermittent slats, not continuous. This breaks up the gusts of wind into harmless eddies and currents. A solid fence simply causes a tidal wave of wind a little further on. Dick Baker had a seven-foot-high solid stone wall all around his vegetable garden, but we can't all be Chief Secretaries.

Having got the essentials of the kitchen garden going, I turned my attention to the hothouse. A few panes needed to be replaced, and all the putty was rotten, but both glass and putty were available from the Public Works Department. I repaired these, and got all the doors and ventilation windows working smoothly, and painted. There was a peat-burning stove at the far end to heat the four-inch water pipes that ran all around the four-foot-high, brick-built, soil troughs. A second water system allowed controlled automatic water-ing of the plants through a continuous pipe winding round all the soil troughs, with tiny holes in it, allowing a gentle seepage of water onto the plant roots. To be really effective, the soil in each trough should be completely removed each summer (it made good topsoil), and replaced with a 50/50 mix of fresh garden soil and horse manure. We were blessed with the racecourse just behind our house, where horses grazed throughout the year. I and the children would spend many a happy evening collecting our manure, and excellent mush-rooms, whilst Hilary prepared the evening meal. Add to this richly scented 50/50 mix a little chicken manure (too much is lethal), and tomatoes, courgettes and calabrese will grow like there is no tomorrow.

So what is missing? Flowers. Scent. Beauty. Colour. The islands are beautiful in a brown/green, Scottish Highlands sort of a way. But something was definitely missing, and I fully recognised what it was when I visited Mr Bennett, the magistrate, at his home. He and his wife had built a huge heated conservatory onto, almost into, their house. It was full of roses, carnations, gladioli, sweet pea, cornflower, and the like. It was an inspiration. At the front of our house we had a large north-facing glass porch, to keep the wind off our front door. We draughtproofed it, waterproofed it, and generally tarted it up. We found somewhere else for all the wellington boots, anoraks and cagoules, and then filled it up with tea chests full of soil, and off we went. Sweet peas, pinks and night-scented stock for fragrance, and marigold, trailing lobelia and many others for colour. It was a tiny patch of heaven on earth. I put a stool in there, and sat there to write my sermons.

Another who gardened with great skill was Monsignor Spraggon. He specialised in gladioli and the Roman Catholic church was resplendent with them. Whenever he wanted to say 'thank you' he would send a bunch for Hilary, knowing that the way to some men's hearts is through their wives. Captain Mike was impressed at our gardening results, and turned his hand to it too. He dug a large patch, and planted it entirely with turnips, a vegetable he is not particularly fond of. He grew a magnificent crop of turnips, probably the best in Stanley. Why he did this turnip thing I have no idea at all. He never tried gardening again. Poor old Harry, the Anglican chaplain, hated gardening, and did not like it at all that I enjoyed mine. Somehow he could not find life, or anything to do with it, a joyful thing. I really do hope he finds heaven as happy a place as I found our front porch, or my lovely London garden now. Hilary says she can find my soul in there, even when life is in its harder moments.

CHAPTER 16

Camping in the Camp

CAMPING ON THE Falkland Islands was quite a challenge. I have already described the joys of sinking gently into bogs in our Land-Rover, and getting out again. Hilary and I could only go off together if there was a visiting doctor, usually from BAS, able to give medical cover for us, so I usually took the children, and sometimes a friend, and sometimes Captain Mike's son, alone. Mike would overfly us from time to time, to see that all was well. Because of the frequent gale force winds, we had to choose the campsites very carefully, usually in a deep, steep-sided valley, protected from the winds. The effort was always worthwhile. The summer weather was usually bright and clear, despite the winds. The children could play on the huge, pure white, sandy beaches, that sloped gently out to the bays of crystal-clear water, whilst I kept an eye on them as I collected large, succulent mussels from the rocks around. We would cook these, along with any fish that the children caught, in seawater on a campfire on the seashore. They all tasted delicious. The mussels often had small, richly-coloured, natural pearls in them, which were a bit scrunchy on the teeth but beautiful to collect and look at. We had to be careful to avoid sunburn whilst camping. In the very clear air, and cooling breezes, it was all too easy to get badly burnt.

We had deliberately chosen low tents that did not catch the wind too much. Each child had his or her own one-man tent. This was kept as tidy or as scruffy, and as private or as public, as each child chose. Having your very own first tent is rather like having your own first home. You can design it and decide how it is going to be for yourself. We each had an electric torch to use at night. The skies were so clear and unpolluted that the stars shone like fiery jewels in the sky. The Southern Cross always dominated, but all the Southern constellations that we never see in Britain were there. But we did miss our familiar Plough, Orion, Canis Major, the Great W, or Cassiopeia, and the rest that dominate the northern skies. We had a single camping gas ring, but it was of little use, as the tents were too small to use it in them safely. We did the bulk of our cooking on campfires of dry

A warm summer's day.

heather and driftwood, between suitably-shaped boulders. I still recall the sweet smell of that heather smoke today.

We had taken a brand new Land-Rover out with us on appointment to the Falklands. We wanted to explore the islands, and we did so, but there was all too little free time to do all we wanted. At the same time, the Royal Marines were underprovided with transport for their exercises. We struck a deal. When they wanted to borrow our vehicle, they were welcome. When we went camping they fitted us out with a reliable radio link back to their base, so that I could always be contacted in a medical emergency at the hospital. Mike would then fly out and pick me up from the nearest bay or lagoon.

Major Garry would often accompany us on camping trips. He adored children, and he took every opportunity to encourage their spirit of adventure. It really was a quite amazing opportunity for any child, and ours loved it. He was Action Man, alive and real. Whilst driving over particularly boggy ground, he would run for miles and miles in front of the vehicle to keep us on firmer terrain. It is much easier to debog a Marine than a Land-Rover. Captain Mike would also join us when he could, being dropped off by a colleague, and picked up again when needed. We would all sit around the campfire,

Waiting at the Beaver shed. Myself, our three children and Mike Selwood's son.

relaxing, drinking and talking, as the exhausted children fell asleep in the firelight. They would then go to their tents, snuggle down into their sleeping bags, and sleep deeply, ready for the next day.

We once had the privilege and the great good fortune to be allowed to use a remote, empty farmhouse out at Volunteers, a pleasant day's drive from Stanley. Between our Rover, and several Beaver flights, we managed to get most of Mike's and our families, and Garry, together to enjoy this beautiful place. It is a long stretch of low sand-dunes and open flat turf, grazed to a fine lawn by geese and sheep. The turf had many hundreds of burrow holes in it, made not by rabbits, of which there were none, but by Magellan Penguins, which nest down them. This is one of the few areas where horses refuse to go, because their hoofs keep falling into the long burrows. Humans are well advised to steer clear of the burrows, because, if you fall over one, mother penguin will come out and give you a good going-over with a large, sharp beak. Seals and sea lions rest and nest on the beaches, where they deliver and suckle their young. We all wandered, amazed, among hundreds of these large sea mammals nursing their young, and thousands of nesting seabirds. We could have touched them, but were advised not to do so, in case it disturbed their nesting. There were two colonies of about two hundred king penguins apiece there. These magnificent birds stand about three feet high, the height of Gwyn, our youngest, at that time. Their coat is of a deep velvety black, with a glistening, pure white apron, set off with splashes of gold on the chest and neck. As we were walking over the turf a pair of males walked over to Gwyn. The three of them, all the same height, inspected each other with care, and, when satisfied, all walked in a row together, hand by flipper, to visit the colony – an impressive and colourful group. Lady King Penguins lay one egg each, once a year. They are large, heavy eggs, about four inches long. She then nudges it with her beak to lie on her outstretched webbed feet. She then stands there, with a huge flap of warm, fat belly skin covering the egg until it hatches a few weeks later. She stands there through frost, wind and snow, in the early spring. Dad will be very busy fishing, returning frequently with a large fish in his beak to keep Mum well nourished.

Now imagine this. Two hundred of these giant birds, all standing still in a small circle, less than thirty yards across, all eating several pounds of raw fish a day. The waste just piles up, a thick, rich, highly-concentrated fish manure in ever increasing layers. Never, never stand down wind of a King Penguin colony. The shags, or cormorants, are not much better. They use the same nesting site again and again, even passing it on from one generation to the next. At least they don't all nest together, but they, also, never leave the nest during incubation. So as the female sits upon her eggs, upon the pile of excrement, it gets higher, and higher. This may give the lady shag better ventilation, but it does nothing for the surrounding atmosphere.

CHAPTER 17

Wildlife

O N ONE MEDICAL visit to Sea Lion Island we had some time to spare, and the pilot, Mike, and I were invited to visit the elephant seals. There was a large colony there for the breeding season, and the young had recently been born. There were about forty mature males, huge beasts, the size of a cow, and rather threatening. Each was guarding his harem of two to eight females, about half the size of the males. Lying on the soft white sand each female was suckling her litter of five or six little dark seal cubs. The little ones were very inquisitive, and kept coming to look at this curious little group of humans visiting them. They would come flipping through the sand to get closer to us. But Dad would give a growling bark, telling them to get back to Mum. If he was not quickly obeyed, he would come lumbering toward us to see us off.

We did not argue. On one picnic we took a pretty, and rather self-conscious lady with us. After lunch she disappeared behind a line of tall rocks for a pee. A minute later she reappeared, running for her life, carrying a pair of bright red nylon knickers in her hand. Behind her, at remarkably high speed, considering his huge bulk, came a very angry bull elephant seal. Mike was with us, and shouted to her to drop the knickers on the ground, and to hide behind a rock. She did so. The bull seal went to examine the knickers, and forgot all about her. She was a bit shaken by the encounter. The moral of this is 'Do not wave a red flag at a bull.' In nature, red is often a danger warning, or a threat of danger.

On another occasion Hilary and the children were invited to visit Seal Bay House for a few days. A young farmer and his wife lived in the house. The nearest settlement was Johnson's Harbour, eight miles away. Four families lived at Johnson's. It was a very pleasant walk from one to the other, and quite safe from getting lost. You simply followed the wire fence the entire distance. I once did the walk in the company of a shepherd, a large flock of sheep, and two sheepdogs, when the sheep were going to Johnson's Harbour for shearing. The top two wires of the fence were used as a telephone line on dry days.

It didn't work in the wet. I was able to join the family there for a few hours. They had been walking, with the farmer's wife, among groups of sea lions, and had been delighted to see hours of display dance/swimming by courting dolphins. They took me to see a sight that is now permanently imprinted on my memory. There was a beach about four miles long, and half a mile wide, in a gently sweeping curve, absolutely covered in nesting Gentoo penguins. I estimated, by making a crude count of penguins per square yard, then multiplying this by the area involved, that we were gazing at about six million birds in one sweep of the eye.

About two years later that colony, and many other penguin colonies were decimated, and only a few thousand were left. Many explanations and theories were put forward, from poisoning by the activities of humans to overfishing of the local fish stocks. I think it perfectly possible that if one of those six million birds caught a serious infection, then it would spread very quickly to all the others, as they were so crowded on that beach. They are recovering their numbers again now.

From home we could walk in a couple of hours straight up from the harbour, gradually gaining height up Tumbledown Mountain, and get a magnificent view over Stanley, its inner harbour, and then the parallel outer harbour. Alternatively we could walk along the river feeding the Moody Brook end of the harbour, the River Murrell. With good green turf on its banks it was a lovely place to picnic, and excellent for fishing. The sea trout would congregate at the river mouth to eat the myriad bits of vegetation that came down in the river water. The Royal Marines set up a simple smoking system and produced large fillets of heather-smoked sea trout. Delicious.

This fish smoking was in the best military tradition of the islands. When the French seized the islands from the British in 1770, they built a large, thick stone-walled garrison fort at Port Louis, their capital. We were privileged to stay in the fort for a few days, visiting the farmer's family that lived in part of the fort in 1981. The walls were so thick that the children could play in the window casements. The French needed food. The fort was near a river outlet. It ran down into a long, narrow, v-shaped bay. Like the Murrell, this river was full of bits of vegetation floating down, which the fish needed. So greedy were the fish, and so narrow the apex of the bay where the river came in, and so many were the fish, that they actually piled up, on top of each other, until they were forced above the water level. It was possible to stand in this fish swarm, and simply kick them ashore to a partner, who could stun them and pack them in sacks. The French had fresh fish and smoked fish ad infinitum. But they only got grey mullet, an undistinguished fish with a faintly muddy flavour. Classy, connoisseur fish were only developed by the Royal Marines, with their heather-smoked sea trout. Rule Britannia.

The man who drowned out the choir with his post-mother's stake voice was a keen fisherman. Perhaps he sang to them, and they came to him in total surrender. Whatever, he caught lots and lots of fish, so many that the seagulls came to take their share. This annoyed him greatly, as the birds became adept at snatching the struggling fish from the end of his fishing line as he reeled them in. His solution was simple. He would lasso two or three birds with his line, bring them in, and ring their necks. He then displayed his victims' corpses to all the other birds as a warning, and the wiser ones kept away. The marines were more direct in scaring off the seagulls. When the birds interfered with their fine line and rod fishing, they would use their SA80 high velocity rifles.

These weapons fire a rather small bullet at very high speed (much faster than the speed of sound, hence their strange-sounding report). When a gull is hit it explodes into a dramatic cloud of feathers. The gulls soon learned to pay proper respect to Her Majesty's Royal Marines.

CHAPTER 18

Fowl and food

I HAVE ALWAYS been very fond of fowl. Hens are far more friendly than most women, and are often much more beautifully attired. Have you ever seen an ugly hen? Cockerels take great pride in their plumage, their posture, and their voices. That is why the French adopted a cockerel as their national symbol, rather as we chose Britannia, a full-figured, well-busted, female. France is great for art, cooking, holidays, but not for anything too serious. We British took procreation far more seriously. In our hands cockerels tended to have pampered lives, surrounded by gorgeous hens, full of good food and their favourite activities, but rather short. Once they really got crowing, we ate them. There is always another one behind.

Ducks are quite fantastic. Again, they have huge pride in their appearance, and they are inquisitive birds. They will watch any person, or activity, from a distance, and size up the situation. How can they best get food, attention or admiration in any particular circumstance? Watch them one day. Parent ducks love to display their young to admiring humans. Drakes are wonderfully oversexed, and will often slip away for a quick one with someone else's duck if they think their partner isn't watching. If he gets away with it, he returns home all cheeky looking, to his own partner, often only to get a good telling-off. And if he gets caught, the uproar beats any human domestic row. Beware ducks in spring, however. The females will choose a circuit, preferably encircling your bedroom. They will then march, in an ordered row, ladies first, then the drakes, round and round their circuit from about 3.30 a.m. until seven or eight in the morning, quacking in unison. The row is terrible, and sleep is impossible. I have yet to find a way to shut them up. At least they don't annoy the neighbours like cockerels do; they stick to torment-ing their own owner.

Geese are quite different again. These huge, handsome birds are very proud. Couples are quite remarkably faithful to each other once they have agreed on a partnership – far more so than humans, or ducks – but they will fly or swim for many miles to find the sweetheart of their choice. On many a spring morning we would wake up to find our entire flock, along with that of the Royal Marines from four miles up the harbour, bobbing up and down in the inner harbour, sorting out their potential matrimonial affairs. Then there were the courting rituals – very, very noisy at dawn at about five in the morning.

All the birds, other than geese in early spring, would return home to their favourite places to sleep each night. This is the time to catch the bird of your choice for dinner next day. Cockerels, hens and ducks are easy to kill. Simply take them firmly by the head, swing them round a couple of times, and they are dead before they know what has happened. Then plunge the body into a bucket of very hot water, and the feathers virtually fall off. (They make an excellent addition to composted manure.) The head is easily removed with ordinary garden secateurs. But a goose? There's not a hope of wringing a goose's neck. They are incredibly strong, big birds, with a very strong will to live. My solution, for what it is worth, is to catch the bird, and straddle it with both legs, keeping the powerful wings against the body of the bird with your legs and knees. Then drawing the head gently back, saying gentle, kind last words to the poor goose, cut the throat very quickly with one sharp, quick movement with a very sharp carving knife. The feelings of guilt and remorse, when the other geese greet you sullenly next morning, are awful. But a goose does make an excellent meal for eight to twelve people. Stuff it well, and cook it slowly in a low oven for at least five hours. Kelpers used to shoot the wild upland geese. These are nearly as tasty as domestic geese, but full of lead shot. The marines shot them with their SA80s. This is great, but you must be a magnificent shot. If you hit the body you 'blow the bugger to bits', as a Kelper so gently put it. The effect is rather like an atomic mushroom cloud, but of feathers more than dust. You must aim for, and hit, either the head or the neck. The marines were very good at it.

All our fowl were fed on fresh grain daily, and the geese grazed the paddock, leaving it a well-manured, deep rich green. I improved the quality by sowing some different grass seeds, recommended by the sheep research scientist. By scattering around a fair weight of horse manure we also benefited from good crops of mushrooms. Symbiosis.

In winter the hens tend to go off the lay unless pampered. Pamper them we did. The trick here is hot mash. All year round they got first pick at the vegetable peelings, before they went on the compost heaps. But in winter these peelings all went into a large tureen, with a little added grain, to be boiled up into a rich vegetable soup. This was served to the hens lukewarm. Hilary is an expert chicken menu chef.

We never kept a pig, although many friends did so, and I was sorely tempted. A previously-appointed lady doctor had kept one, and the neighbours complained incessantly as it did not smell too good. I think this was probably her fault, not the pig's. Pigs are handsome, pigs are clever, however, just to prove this rule, one sometimes meets one who . . . sorry, Roald Dahl. This pig did smell. All it needed was a decent place to bath. Pigs like to be clean. They teach their young excellent toilet hygiene. If a pig smells then blame the owner, not the pig. The marines had two pigs. The slaughtering of a pig was a time of anxious negotiation. Friends and neighbours could barter for a quarter, an eighth, or a sixteenth with whatever treasure they had. Money didn't come into it. We offered prime fish, given to us by the Polish deep-sea trawler men. We got enough for three or four good parties.

Cows were regularly slaughtered on the camp farms, and could be bought by the quarter. Quarter cow, that is. But that was just the start of the problem. You had to arrange transport of your quarter cow by sea, on the MV *Forrest*. It was far too heavy for our little aeroplanes. The slaughter would always be timed to coincide with a visit of the ship to that settlement. It would then be delivered by truck, to the pavement outside your house, by the harbourmaster. (He was a great chap. I kept his migraine under control, and he didn't moan too much about our drinking the Royal Marines' duty-free gin.) You then had to get a group of neighbours to help heave this quarter of a cow into a suitable shed to butcher it. Being a doctor, I was advised to butcher it myself, as no one was better trained. It was two weekends' worth of very hard work with cleaver, meat saw, and a huge long butcher's knife. The spoils were shared among all who had helped with provision, transport, butchering and labour, and our huge deep-freeze was well stocked with very welcome beef.

CHAPTER 19

Practice life

THERE WAS NO ready-made entertainment on the islands. A film was shown fortnightly in the village hall. There were annual horse races. There were sheepdog trials. We went once. Sheep and dogs disappeared over the horizon, not to be seen again that day. There were three pubs and that was about it. There was no television but the local radio station did a sterling job with a staff of two, headed by Mr Watts. They rebroadcast BBC World Service, and gave bulletins of local news, including the aeroplane flights for that day, and the passenger lists, so that passengers could be in the right rowing boat at the right place at the right time, or on the correct pier or landing strip. On one memorable occasion the first headline announcement of local news was that the Haines's cat Mandla was missing. He had been away for two days, and he was not with Suzy Wong. The broadcast was quickly followed up with a call from one of the pubs. He had gone out drinking with some Royal Marines, and was enjoying himself. I was a little embarrassed. The cat was a great wanderer. He regularly turned up at the hospital, and at the children's school. He would simply follow us there. At school he would be given a cushion for the day. He also spent much time at the police station with Toddy, and at Moody Brook with the marines. He managed to get into the Governor's secret cipher safe one day. I was summoned to come and remove him forthwith. Silly man shouldn't have left the door open, should he?

The best entertainment of all on the islands was free, and regularly available. It was the daily half-hour radio medical clinic. Everyone, but everyone, tuned in. Hilary or I would spend half an hour in the radio shed with Eileen Vidal, the operator. She had married a Chilean, and she knew a thing or two about the brutal regime then in place under General Pinochet. Her daughter was in Tudor's class at school, and they were great friends. Eileen often used to warn me that the Argentines would come one day and I laughed at her. Later I found her to be a very brave woman. During these radio clinics we would check with each settlement in turn, in a set order —

what medical problems they had, who had missed a period, who was constipated, who had chest pain, what was the pain like, sharp or dull, where did it radiate to, was it associated with exercise, were there any other symptoms. A detailed discussion on treating someone's piles, athlete's foot, or warts would follow. Rashes were always interesting to try and diagnose over the radio and every word of this was listened to on every radio set in the islands. It was wonderful entertainment.

Having made a radio diagnosis, the doctor would prescribe over the radio. Every settlement had a well-stocked medicine chest full of drugs and dressings. We could prescribe from these over the radio, and then arrange to replace the items used by airdrop. Bottles of medicine dropped badly, even when well padded with bubble film. Each settlement had someone who took the lead in health matters, and we worked closely with them. We taught simple suturing of minor lacerations, and injection techniques, as well as basic first aid. It was often the settlement manager's wife who took on these duties, and they were very good at it. When we did Camp medical visits we would usually use their main front room as our clinic. The only problem with this resupply system was after a serious drinking bout. The hung-over drinker would try to put off the hangover and the vomiting with drugs taken from the medicine chest without permission. These were then unavailable for legitimate use. We soon sussed out the main culprits, and muttered things to them about the Black List.

Sometimes Hilary and I would discuss a case with each other over the radio, when one of us was in Camp and the other in Stanley. In order to preserve some confidentiality we used to talk in SiSwati, which we had learnt in Swaziland. This certainly foxed the listeners-in, but it had the unfortunate effect of convincing the patient that death was imminent. We did have one very frightening case to discuss, both for the patient, and for us too. Hilary admitted a Polish seaman with a high fever. I was out in the Camp somewhere, and she did all the usual tests and investigations. We discussed him at length, and got nowhere. He was a little better next day, the fever dropped, and we thought it might just be some obscure Polish virus, perhaps influenza. However, the next day he deteriorated again, developed an even higher fever, and was fighting for his life. Father Moynihan came in to give him the last rites.

Hilary was staring, bewildered as we both were, at his pulse, temperature, respiration and blood pressure chart. We were reminded of typhoid, malaria and scarlet fever patterns, which we had known so well in Swaziland. But this was a Pole, in the Falkland Islands. We asked if he had ever been to Africa, through our refugee interpreter, and were told 'No, definitely not.' We continued our ward round, when an auxiliary rushed in with a scribbled note. 'Dakar. Four hours. Changed ship.' That was it. His fever was rising horribly, perhaps for the last time. We took more blood, and our wonderful laboratory technician stained it and found it teeming with all stages of malignant falciparum malaria. We had no antimalarial drugs whatsoever in the hospital stores, and it would take at least a few days to get some flown out from Britain or the Argentine. So we turned to Martindale. This huge volume is to pharmacy what Gray's *Anatomy* is to anatomists, a definitive text. And we found a brilliant section on what useful drugs for malaria you might have available if you had no conventional antimalarials. Precisely our situation. He made a slow, but complete recovery, and went back to sea a very happy trawlerman.

Books were very useful in that hospital. Whenever I operated I had a copy of Hamilton Bailey's *Emergency and Operative Surgery* on a music stand beside me, with an auxiliary nurse to turn the pages as we went through each operation. It was a great aide memoire in the more complicated procedures, and mentioned all the common problems and anatomical variations likely to be met during any operation, and how to deal with them. Our textbook on toxic pharmacology (poisoning) was a godsend, too. Whatever should you do when a child mixes a little sheep-dip with orangeade, and gives it to a friend? Look it up. Answer: pump out the stomach, force diuresis, and pray. It worked.

CHAPTER 20

Autumn 1982

A ND SO LIFE went on week by week, flying past all too fast. Being comfortably busy with medical work, Camp medicine, gardening, dinner parties and camping trips, there was little free time left. We had intended to do a three-year tour on the islands, with a mid-tour break in the Falkland midwinter, the English mid-summer, based back in our permanent home in London.

The annual changeover of the Royal Marine Naval Party was about to take place. We knew we were going to lose Major Noott, whose company we had all enjoyed so much. He was going to be with his wife and daughters again. Life was never dull with him around, even at the cathedral. One of our regular congregation there was a splendidly mad old lady. Garry would always offer her a lift home after services there, in the battered old marines' Land-Rover. She was schizophrenic, but had wonderfully vivid and well-ordered delusions. These centred on a machiavellian plot, orchestrated by Old Harry, the chaplain. She was convinced that Harry had recruited some Argentines living in Stanley to capture and dramatically dispose of the Governor. (Would that they had!). At the end of evensong on Sundays she was to be seen crouching and scurrying around Garry's Rover, watching the Governor go to his official car, a maroon-coloured London taxi, with a crown instead of a number plate, and a small Union Jack flying from a pennant. Very posh. As she carried out her covert, protective prowl around the Rover, so Garry could often be seen creeping around behind her, marine-style, hoping to keep her out of real trouble. He was concerned for her physical, as well as mental, well-being, and he really did not want her causing an international incident by skewering some unsuspecting Argentine with her trusty umbrella. So losing Garry was going to be a blow, but we knew his successor from a previous visit of his, and one marine officer is likely to be as lively as another. HMS *Endurance* arrived with the new naval party of marines, and the two Lynx helicopters flew repeatedly from the ship to Moody Brook, re-supplying the marines. All that gin had to come from somewhere.

HEGFI's official car, a maroon London taxi.

The inner harbour was too shallow at the Moody Brook end for the *Endurance* to go up there.

March 1982 was a pleasant autumn month. The hens had laid well, and we had a surplus of eggs preserved in a large bucket of alum, or isinglass. The vegetable garden was well stocked with greens and root crops. We had several sacks of potatoes in the dry store ready for the winter. The hothouse was producing enough and to spare. We had a large, secure supply of dry peat in a shed. The geese and ducks were heavy with their winter fat. The geese actually form a heavy keel of fat under the belly as a winter store for energy and for insulation against the cold. Much of it is used by the lady geese when they sit on their eggs in spring. As they waddle along in winter they look rather like a ship out of water. We could always see how well they were doing when we took off or landed in the Beaver float plane, because the flight path was along the harbour front, and we had a superb view of our own paddock.

We arranged a farewell dinner for Garry – the usual four of us, our wives and a swarm of children. It was a very good meal, but there was a curious tension in the air, which I could not properly understand. It was 31 March. Somehow Dick Baker and Garry Noott were not at their usual ease. There was much talk on the BBC World

Service about some Argentine scrap-metal merchants making trouble on an Antarctic base, one of the BAS stations that used to be an old whaling station. HMS *Endurance* had gone to sort them out. The Argentines kept claiming the Falkland Islands as their own because they are only three hundred miles from their coast. (That argument gives Britain fair claim on France, Holland, Belgium and Germany. Perhaps we should try it.) The Kelpers would have none of it. The Argentines had hyperinflation and a foul military dictatorship that used to 'disappear' around two thousand people a year for not agreeing with them, and that was more than the entire population of the islands put together. I thought that all this, and waiting to get home to his wife and children, was making Garry a bit tense. Little did I know that he and Dick Baker had had the first warnings from the Foreign Office in London that things might be about to go horribly wrong. Dinner ended. We all departed, a little sad, a little bewildered.

The next day dawned bright and beautiful as ever, with the clear yellow gold sunlight pouring in through our east-facing bedroom window. We were up as ever to rake the boiler, feed the fowl, adjust the hothouse water, and make the first cups of tea for the family. All were up to breakfast and the children ready for school, bicycles checked for the one-mile harbourside ride to school watched over by a giant petrel. It must be one of the most beautiful rides to school that any child has ever had, and an ornithologist's paradise. Hilary and I had an ordinary sort of a day at the hospital. Everything was normal, until 4.30 p.m., when I got a rather curt call from the Governor's secretary, telling me to go directly to the Governor's office, for a 5 p.m. meeting. I walked the half a mile, wondering what was on His Excellency's mind, and met the Director of Education on his way to the same meeting. Neither of us had instigated the meeting, and we wondered if the little man had had some bright new idea about health education. This might be interesting!

PART III

CHAPTER 21

The War or, in politically correct language, the South Atlantic Conflict

W E WERE NOT greeted by any bright idea. The Governor had called in all the heads of department to tell us that he had received information from Britain that a small, but significant flotilla of Argentine warships were a few miles off the Falkland coast. They were clearly visible and identifiable from satellite photographs. There was no possible reason for them to be there other than either to pose a threat of an invasion of the Falkland Islands, or actually to do it. In the event of actual invasion, he told us, he had instructed the Royal Marines' Naval Party to resist with all possible force. I was to prepare the hospital for mass casualties.

This was the problem, and the challenge, of a lifetime. We had a small GP hospital with eleven general beds, three maternity beds, ten geriatric beds, a tiny operating theatre and a very small staff. On the plus side we did have three to six months supplies, at normal rates of use, of drugs, dressings and intravenous fluids. All the staff worked like beavers that evening and night. We made the operating theatre ready. We arranged all our emergency drugs and intravenous fluids in convenient positions for ready access. We sent home all the inpatients that we possibly could. I had my own sizeable office, with its posh person's loo, and official government rubber stamp 'Office of the Senior Medical Officer'. Nearby was the staff duty room. We brought our three children to sleep with Hilary and myself between these two rooms. By 2 a.m. we had made all the preparations that we could think of, and we all tried to settle down to sleep. It was not easy.

How could this be happening to us? And to our lovely, peaceful islands? We knew the Argentines had some bad habits, like 'disappearing' people, and we were not overfond of their military government. Nevertheless, we were very fond of some individual Argentines. One had almost been part of our family in the Cayman Islands. We had known about the 'scrap metal merchants' on South Georgia. Only later did we learn that they were actually a force of Argentine commandos, led by an officer, Alfredo Astiz, who was reputed to have delighted in murdering nuns. He was not the nicest of Argentine men. I recalled that Eileen Vidal, the radio operator with whom we did our morning Camp radio clinics, had often warned me that the Argentines might well be mad enough to come one day. But we had laughed about it. They wouldn't, would they? Britain was known to be quite keen to give them the Falkland Islands. They were an expensive embarrassment to post-colonial Britain. It was only the loud voices of the Kelpers themselves that was causing the delay.

There was an armed flotilla, a few miles out to sea. One of the pilots had gone out to have a look. Not too close, but yes, they were there. The garden of Government House was ablaze with burning secret diplomatic and cipher papers. This was just across the football field, in front of my office window. The threat was obviously being taken seriously. The Governor told all the population what was going on over the radio, which Patrick Watts kept going all night. Everyone was told to bunker down, as best they could. There might be actual fighting, bullets flying, around their little wooden houses. The duty room, and my office, were built with double thickness breeze-block walls – enough to slow, but not to stop, a modern high-velocity rifle bullet. We felt relatively safe. But it was a strange, unreal feeling, more disbelief than worry. In the few hours from 5 p.m. to 2 a.m. our situation had changed from a very steady, solid, predictable way of life to a prolonged frenzy of activity that we could not really comprehend or believe.

A minor emergency occurred. The ambulance driver-cum-mortuary attendant-cum second gardener had gone absent without leave. He left a message that he was not driving the ambulance with people shooting around him. He was going to the Camp. I had to let Garry, who was just a little busy at this stage, know about this. He accepted the situation with very good grace, and sent a Royal Marine to collect the ambulance. He was expecting serious casualties. Then there was another upset. One of the less mentally stable of our young ladies was so upset by the news of a possible invasion that she went completely berserk. It was the very last thing we needed at that time. I gave her a very large injection of chlorpromazine in her derrière, and left her to sleep it off in one of our very seriously needed beds. I put her in the padded drying-out ward bed and thought a few rather unkind thoughts about her that night.

But now it was 2 a.m. on Friday, 2 April, 1982. I was satisfied that we had done everything we could to prepare for what we hoped would not happen. I had been twenty years in the Territorial Army, mostly as a dental officer, and had had rather more training than most general practitioners in setting up emergency medical facilities in the field. But that was all practice and training, not the real thing. However, at least it set the mind running along the right tracks. Reception. Triage. Resuscitation. Surgery. Recovery. Nursing. Evacuation. A workable circuit must be in place. Medical supplies must be strategically placed. Each individual must know their job, their duties, and what was expected of them. Like fun, in a little, remote GP hospital. But we did our best. Our children, now aged 9, 7 and 4, took it all very well. We told them the truth of what was happening, and in all the detail that we knew. We answered their questions as honestly and as fully as we could. I think to this day that our forthright honesty with them on that night, and each night thereafter, actually carried them through their ordeal without too much mental damage, or post-traumatic stress syndrome, as it is politically-correctly called today. They went quite soundly asleep. So sound asleep that they did not hear the first mortar shells exploding in the distance at 4 a.m. that morning.

CHAPTER 22

The first morning

I MUST HAVE slept very badly that night. I kept dreaming that I was
on a Territorial Army exercise, that there was live mortar fire in the
exercise, and that I was soon to be shaken awake by my sergeant,
ready as always with a cup of hot, sweet tea. Suddenly, horribly, it
dawned on me that this was no exercise. This was the real bloody
thing. People were going to get hurt. Badly hurt. And my lovely little
GP hospital was the only medical facility we had. O, Christ! What a
responsibility. I shared it with Him for a few moments. I had slept in
my underclothes and socks (all clean), a trick I had learnt serving with
the Army. It makes it much quicker, easier and warmer to get out of
bed and fully dressed for action. I went to peer out of my office
windows. They faced Government House in one direction, and the
front hospital garden, and the slope down to the harbour in the other.
The street lighting was adequate. My night vision is good. I could see
nothing abnormal, but I could hear the unmistakable sound of mortar
fire a little closer than before. A first, sharp, explosive, crack of a
sound, as the mortar shell is fired from the tube, then, ten seconds to
half a minute later, a dull crump of an explosion, as the mortar shell
arrives at its destination. Where? What were the bastards shelling? We
only had eighty Royal Marines fighting them. You don't fire a mortar
shell at an individual soldier; you use a rifle for that. You use a mortar
to take out a vehicle, a machine-gun post, a defended trench, or
perhaps a building. Were they mortaring the homesteads on the
airport road? That is where the sound appeared to be coming from.
There was still no movement around the hospital that I could see.

I put on the kettle for that hot, sweet tea that I had been dreaming
of and took a cup to Hilary and to the senior nurse, and woke them
with the awful news. Someone turned on the radio. It was going
non-stop. Patrick, the reporter, was taking telephone calls from the
houses that the Argentines were passing through, and broadcasting
them live to all the islands. It appeared that they had invaded
somewhere near the airport and were coming in that way. Then
another lot came in from another beach in the Bluff Cove direction

in a pincer movement. No, the Argentines were not mortaring buildings deliberately, which was some comfort. They hit and destroyed one by mistake, but the occupants had already fled. A number of armoured personnel carriers were reported to be approaching Stanley, firing intermittently with their machine guns, at nothing in particular. Perhaps the mortars were doing likewise, making a lot of noise and showing off their fire power just for the hell of it and to intimidate their opposition. Then I saw a slight movement in the cabbage patch in the front of the hospital garden. It was a Royal Marine, moving forward, towards Government House. Two others, behind, were giving him cover. Then one by one each of the three moved forward towards their destination, at all times the moving marine being covered by the two others. They were retreating from the invasion coasts where they had been, back towards Government House. Suddenly a machine gun opened up from behind me. I slipped to the back of the hospital, and looked out of a storeroom window. Dawn was about to break, but it was still dark. There was a machine-gun crew set up behind my mortuary, in the hospital garden. They were using one in five tracer, ranging in on the near hedge of Government House. Machine guns are fed their bullets, or rounds, in long chains. One in five tracer contains four standard rounds followed by one tracer round repeatedly. The tracer round flares like a firework rocket as it travels with the others to its target. Thus you can see exactly what you are hitting with the standard rounds. It can be a very beautiful sight, but in this case it was terrifying. The three Royal Marines had been making straight for that hedge. I watched as long as I could, but saw no one get hit. Then, from behind the hospital, a man started screaming in pain. He had clearly been hit. His screams quickly died down, as his life ebbed away. Was it a marine, or an Argentine? Screams have no language. It was sickening.

I saw no more Royal Marines that day. Just more and more Argentines moving towards, and surrounding, Government House. For the ill-disciplined savages that I thought them, they were actually doing quite well. Three thousand Argentines had overcome eighty of our marines. Then they brought up the mortars. They ranged these in around Government House. All our marines had retreated there to form a final defence for the Governor. He kept coming up on the radio, saying that the marines were defending him bravely. It was obvious to an imbecile that they were totally surrounded, and could be eliminated at will at any moment. I heard later that this ridiculous situation was brought to an end when an Argentine lobbed a hand grenade into the room where His Excellency and Major Noott and others were holed up. Major Noott hurled it straight out again, and then it exploded. That, apparently, brought the great man to his senses. He came on the radio again, saying he was ready to surrender. But how? He had no telephone line to the enemy. He asked anyone among the Argentine forces who was listening to him on the radio to tell their officers that they were ready to surrender to this obviously overwhelming force. No one was listening. Rounds and mortars still kept coming all around them, but not actually at them. It was like a cat playing with a mouse. It was a situation of complete, tragic farce. An army of Argentines and the Governor had got themselves into a situation that they could not get out of. One might have thought that one final round through the right individual might have been an act of mercy to the world. But it was not to be.

Now, many years later, sitting in comfort on top of a North Cyprus mountain, I realise that my language and opinions have become a little strong, both about the Governor, and about the Argentines. Him first. He appeared to me to be playing with the lives of loyal British Royal Marines. I found that, and still do find that very hard to forgive. However, he had been a respected Battle of Britain pilot. And his mother, and God, must have loved him. In fairness, I think he thought as little of me as I of him. Perhaps we are both correct in our mutual estimates of each other. As for the Argentines, it is not the ordinary people that I despise. It is their military junta, their murderous suppression of their own people at that time, and their revolting behaviour on our islands that make me a little indelicate in my writing about them. What I am actually doing is recalling as accurately as I now can what it was like to be that person, me, in that place at that time. So – sorry, but I think it has to be.

CHAPTER 23

The surrender

THE SAVIOUR of the situation was an Argentine spy called Hector. Hector had been head of the Argentine air service between Comodoro Rivadavia and Stanley. This was a weekly flight in an Argentine military transport aircraft. He lived in a large, smart house just a few hundred yards from our own. He was the senior Argentine representative on the Falkland Islands, and was a senior officer in their air force. Incidentally, he had provided the Argentine intelligence services with a very detailed description and assessment of every person of any importance on the islands, whether in local government, the Defence Force, the Executive, or in the Camp – their work, hobbies, income and interests. More of that later. So, in short Hector was a professional spy. A very suave, polite and diplomatic spy to be sure, but he had been spying on us, to prepare for just such an eventuality as this, since his arrival on the islands.

So Hector the Spy was stuck rather uncomfortably at home realising that his Dago military junta of the Argentine, and our Governor, had really cocked it up between them. He asked an Argentine officer, by his own means of communication, whether a surrender would now be acceptable. Certainly it was! So we had a white flag party. I saw them walking from Government House, past the hospital, to the Secretariat, now in enemy hands. I cannot recall now with certainty, but I think it consisted of Dick Baker, the Deputy Governor, Major Noott, Hector the Spy and someone else. They walked past carrying a white flag (what appeared to be a pillow case on a broomstick) to meet the Argentines. It was a curious and rather ludicrous sight, in a crazy situation. If it had not been so tragic a situation it would have been high comedy.

There was a familiar sound of a Land-Rover engine at the back of the hospital. Every Land-Rover had a rather distinctive engine sound, according to its state of maintenance, the number of cylinders functioning properly, and the state of the exhaust. This was the milkman's Rover. I could hardly believe it, but it was him all right. One cylinder fired a little late in the sequence, causing a sound like a

The milk delivery, and F52, on 2 April, 1982.

galloping horse. And there he was, a stolid Kelper farmer, who kept a fine herd of cows. He delivered a gallon of milk to the hospital every day. I went to have a look. He had come on his round as usual, invasion or no invasion. His only acknowledgement of the situation was that he had fixed a pillow case onto a stick, flapping out of one window. There were the usual boxes full of pint plastic bags full of milk in the back of his Rover. He himself was walking down the path carrying eight bags of fresh milk, past the mortuary, past the machine gun emplacement, to the back door of the hospital. The machine gun crew looked on, bemused. He gave his usual 'Good morning, Doc!' and on he went. He did every delivery that day.

My raving pacifist lady, whom I had sedated rather heavily the previous night, woke and started up again. She got a further whack of chlorpromazine in her backside. Not a good way to treat a pretty lady's bottom, but I had no time for cognitive behavioural therapy just then. The staff had prepared a normal, nourishing breakfast. I sat down with them and my family and took the opportunity to enjoy a good meal, as every soldier should. You never know when the next might be. I used the time to explain to our senior nurses how I saw the situation. I thought there must be several horribly wounded Royal Marines out there, men we had treated and cared for over the last year. There must also be a number of horribly maimed and mutilated Argentines, judging from the gunfights of the night. I explained that, under the terms of the Geneva Articles and Conventions, all the wounded must be treated alike, strictly according to their medical needs. I emphasised that we, the medical staff, must be seen to treat the enemy well and professionally, because only then could we claim full protection under the Conventions for our patients and ourselves. We all agreed. We would all try to act in an exemplary manner in these matters.

Sudden panic. One of our nurses was missing, nowhere to be seen. She turned up a bit later, looking rather sheepish. Fearing the worst, she had gone off to sacrifice her virginity with another Government employee, before it was too late. Naughty girl. Naughty boy. The telephone rang. It was the Governor wanting me. The Argentines had accepted his surrender, and there was a ceasefire. There was still an awful lot of firing going on, but I wasn't to worry about that. The mortars had at least stopped. There were two severely wounded Argentines near the road behind the hospital. Would I go and get them? I had no ambulance – it was still off with the marines. (It had been shot up, but continued to function well. Good old Land-Rover ambulance. We got it back after the war, looking like a piece from a gangster film, with fine bullet holes in it.) So I put on a hospital white coat. Hilary put big red crosses front and back, in red adhesive tape. I carried two standard stretchers, and left by the back door of the hospital. At least the machine-gun crew were familiar with me by now. Then I started up the road, feeling rather self-conscious, and horribly exposed. I was shown where to go by shouts and gestures from the Argentines. There were indeed two horribly wounded Argentines there. I signed for their fellow soldiers to put them onto the stretchers, and carry them down to the hospital with me. I wondered and wondered, 'Where are the Marines?'

CHAPTER 24

Paddling in blood

WHAT HAPPENED NEXT cannot be adequately described in words. Had we been able to record it on film, it would probably be dismissed as faked. We actually had a sort of a mad blood-bath in our operating theatre. We had our two operating tables set up, and our two anaesthetic machines going quite well, supplied with oxygen from the Cardiff concentrators, and with halothane as the main anaesthetic agent, old-fashioned but effective, and we were familiar and safe with it. The Argentines had two 'military surgeons', but no anaesthetists. As we were getting sorted, a third wounded Argentine was brought in, with a high-velocity bullet wound to his leg. The two whose collection I had organised had, in one case, a lung wound, and in the other liver and bowel wounds. Whilst we were operating another was brought in with torrential bleeding from a femoral artery wound. We were full to overflowing, and he was taken off by helicopter to one of the Argentine ships that had a medical facility on board.

I thought it best to let the 'surgeons' do the surgery, whilst Hilary and I looked after the anaesthetics, and helped as best we could. Being somewhat individual, and a little temperamental, the anaesthetic machines needed careful monitoring to be safe. Hilary was the most experienced with them because I usually did the surgery, but we had developed our operating techniques together over the years, and I had done plenty of anaesthetics in a previous appointment in the Cayman Islands. Our first, and worst problem, was that of middle-ranking Argentine officers bursting into our tiny operating theatre in full, dirty fighting gear. One actually came in brandishing a general purpose machine gun, not a small weapon. Others were festooned with hand grenades and throwing grenades. All were caked in mud, and the general grime of war. They shouted at the Argentine doctors, and at Hilary and myself, alike, in Spanish. Apparently they wanted us to work more quickly, because of others needing attention. Some of them actually fiddled with the controls of our oxygen concentrators and the anaesthetic machines, turning everything to maximum, to

82

speed things up. This ruined the delicate balances within which each one worked. It was by great good fortune, as well as superb, quiet professionalism, that Hilary was able to retrieve each disastrous situation as it arose. The chap with the chest and lung wounds was the most ill. He was easy enough to anaesthetise. He was dying, and did so with good grace shortly after he was asleep. The Argentine officers immediately accused us of killing him. Very helpful. The man with the liver and abdominal wounds was successfully anaesthetised and stabilised, despite the fact that his metal identification disc, or dog tag as it is called, clearly described him as being blood group A, rhesus positive. In fact, on emergency grouping in our laboratory, he was group O positive. We really would have helped kill him if we had given him group A blood.

The next task was to get the filthy, muddy uniforms off. The padded combat camouflage material is very difficult to cut with anything other than purpose-designed shears, which we did not have. Our nurses had always prepared our patients for surgery in those beautiful, green, sexy nightgown things called operating shirts, which are easy to remove from the patients once they are asleep. Getting the combat uniforms off was very hard work, using the scissors that we had. The 'military surgeon' made an adequate abdominal incision. Inside were several small liver lacerations, bleeding fast, as they do. But the patient also had multiple lacerations of both small and large bowel. The liver wounds were stabilised, and oversewn. The surgeon then carefully sewed up each of the lacerations in the small and large bowel, despite areas of black, non-viable (or dead) bowel, and a large amount of free faeces in the abdominal cavity. For that poor patient to have had a chance of survival he should have had a simple ileostomy, bringing the small bowel to the surface of the abdominal wall, where it could function until the rest of the bowel had healed, and the infection had been overcome. Had that been done he might possibly have survived. Not so. Every laceration was sewn up, the abdominal wall closed, and he was left with a grossly faecally-contaminated abdominal cavity, with a sure certainty of death from septicaemia and toxic shock. I would expect a first-year surgical trainee houseman to know that much.

Our other wonderful 'military surgeon' dealt with the shattered lower leg. He was certainly a technically competent taxidermist, even if he was no surgeon. The first rule with a gunshot wound is to lay it wide open and keep it open for some days. Then all dead tissue, and tissues that have lost their blood supply, should be removed, along with any exterior dirt and shreds of clothing that have been sucked into the wound. Any fragments of bone that have lost their blood supply will simply die and cause infection. They must be removed. The wound is washed thoroughly, and then left open so any pus and further dead tissues can be removed easily. Only when you have a clean, healthy-looking wound, with growth of new, healing tissue in it, should the wound be closed. Our hero put every spicule of bone back in place, dead or alive, like a jigsaw puzzle. He did not disturb his artistic arrangement with surgical lavage, to remove the mud and clothing from within the wound. He carefully stretched the remaining skin over the wound, and sewed it all up very neatly. It looked very good, externally. I have no doubt whatsoever that that Argentine soldier lost either his leg or his life as a result of that 'surgery', quite without necessity. Both these wounded soldiers were evacuated back to the Argentine next day. If the leg injury survived with his life, then I wish him well.

We had still not seen any wounded Royal Marines.

CHAPTER 25

That Friday

A FTER THE BUTCHERY in our operating theatre I got to my radio. I wanted to know if the world knew what was going on in our remote South Atlantic home. By great good fortune we had brought out with us, to the islands, a very powerful, state-of-the-art radio receiver. It has ten short wavebands, each with expanded tuning in the prime areas, as well at the usual long-wave, medium-wave, and very high frequency bands. With this advanced short-wave facility, we could virtually always get BBC World Service, relayed from Ascension Island, over three thousand miles away. We had to adjust the wave length through the day to get the best reception, which was never perfect, but was good enough to hear what was being said. I listened to the news, and to my great relief it was on an almost non-stop emergency broadcast about the invasion of our islands. The BBC reporters had been relayed the Falkland Islands Radio broadcast by an interested amateur. The world was stunned by the news. Then we heard the good news. Despite the Argentine invasion force of three thousand Argentine 'marines' facing a defending force of eighty Royal Marines, we had not suffered a single death or serious injury. I was frankly jubilant, and told all our staff the good news. We had all been very close to our marines. They were good company, even if rather naughty and belligerent at times. Many of us felt rather proprietorial towards them. And now they were all alive and well.

That afternoon a group of Argentine generals, air commodores and admirals came to thank the hospital staff for what we had done for their wounded soldiers. A constant stream of other wounded had continued to come through, and all I can recall now is the blood, the mess, and the gross medical incompetence of their surgeons. However, I accepted their thanks on behalf of the hospital staff politely, and talked to them about the Geneva Conventions. Yes, they had heard of them. (It was only after the war that I found that they were not signatory to the conventions. They never admitted that to me!) Yes, they agreed that I could see and examine all the Royal Marines that they had captured. Yes, they would act in every proper and legal

85

way possible. Yes, our civilians would have every legal right and protection under the conventions. So far, so good, I thought. Little did I know.

The first public act the Argentines did that day was to expel the Governor. He went off to the airport, now an Argentine military airport, in his full Governor's regalia of tailed coat and cocked hat with white feathers in it, in his official personal transport, the maroon London taxi cab. It was a right farce of a sight. So the remaining senior government officer was Dick Baker, the Deputy Governor, a measured, experienced, and reasonable man. We had been next-door neighbours for the previous two years. The senior elected politician around was Mr Monk, a retired sheep farm manager, I believe. Dick Baker was only allowed to remain with us for a few days before he too was expelled from the islands.

Once the military violence of the invasion of the islands was over, we had to contend with its effects on the civilian population. It was the greatest shock to the fabric of Kelper society that had ever been known. A good many, including several with senior positions in Stanley, simply fled to the Camp settlements, and stayed in the smaller settlements where there was little Argentine presence. We lost police officers, teachers, utility workers, and our ambulance driver thus. Those who remained were confused and disturbed. My manic lady patient in the hospital was thankfully taken away by the Argentines back whence she came. I was grateful for that.

One of the geriatric residents of the hospital was profoundly deaf, and did not take in the fact of the invasion at all. She did comment that the plane was noisy today, and there must be an extra flight, because the regular flight was on Tuesdays, not Fridays. (In fact they were Argentine Super Etendards, supersonic fighters built by the French, swooping in pairs low over the harbour.) Whatever, come 10 o'clock that morning she went off, as she did every Friday morning, though this time past dozens of Argentine conscripts, to collect her pension. Eventually a very confused Argentine officer, who had taken over the Post Office, called in the Postmaster General, a kindly fellow, who firmly marched the old lady back into our care, and gave her her pension money out of his own pocket, just to keep the peace. Another of our more loopy residents took it into her mind to see off the Argentines herself. She fixed a small, paper Union Jack onto the viciously pointed tip of her neatly-furled umbrella, and marched up the road saying 'I'll show 'em. I'll fly the Jack!' She had to be hurriedly rescued. She really could have injured someone with her old brolly.

By evening I was exhausted. I took a break, and walked the beautiful harbourside mile back to our home. As I passed Government House I saw all our Royal Marines, lying face down on the front lawn, under arrest. It was a sickening sight, but at least they were all alive and well. I got home, and found a lovely old lady there who often stayed with our children at night when both Hilary and I were needed at the hospital together for a major operation. She had guessed we were all there, and had come to feed the chickens and Mandla, the cat, and to see that our house was in order. Wonderful.

Early the next day I requested, and obtained, permission to see our Marines, one at a time, in privacy in the police station. I was able to check that none had been seriously harmed, and none had any particular medical needs. This was quite straightforward, but I was alarmed by a most sinister character who was watching over them. He was a certain Major Dowling. He was clearly furious that I had got permission to see them privately, and said so. I tried to explain prisoners' rights within the Geneva Conventions, but he was not interested. He then picked up a football that he must have kept for the purpose, and kicked it extremely hard at the station yard wall. He then looked at my head, not saying a word, but clearly implying that he would love to kick it likewise. Nice man. I later learnt that he was a key player in the lovable Argentine death squads, that 'disappeared' about two thousand of their own people a year. He had taken over the office at the front of the police station as his own. It had a lovely view over the inner harbour, to the spit of land that divided inner from outer harbour. More of that later.

I had at home, among my papers, my Royal Commission, a paper from the Queen, acknowledging me to be a 'loyal and trusted soldier', and appointing me a captain in then Royal Army Dental Corps. I was proud of it, and strengthened by it. I took it back to the hospital and pinned it up in my office behind my desk, where every visiting Argentine who came to see me would be faced by it.

CHAPTER 26

The cat's view

THE CAT, Mandla, was loved by the children. Our first kitten on the islands had died a few days after we got him, from a chest infection and asthma. Months later I was called to see a seriously ill old lady in the Camp. An emergency flight was arranged. Catherine, our daughter, asked me what the problem was. I told her it was a serious case of asthma. She considered this carefully, and finally dismissed me with 'I hope you do better for her than you did for my cat.' I felt a little chastened. When Mandla arrived the vet gave him a prophylactic (preventative) course of tetracycline, a broad spectrum antibiotic, and he survived the Haines family germ centre, and thrived. Mandla did not approve of the invasion. As Hilary and the children walked past Government House front lawn next morning, where the Marines had been the previous afternoon and which had subsequently been mined and barricaded with rolls and rolls of barbed wire, down strolled Mandla. The three children all shouted excitedly, 'Mandla, Mandla, come here! And don't step on the mines!' A score of agitated Argentines trained their guns on the cat, and on my family. Mandla walked sedately down the lawn, through the rolls of barbed wire, and was graciously pleased to be picked up by Catherine. Hilary breathed again. Catherine told him not to go with those nasty people again.

Later on that next day after the invasion it became increasingly clear, over the BBC World Service, that Mrs Thatcher, the Prime Minister of Great Britain with a handbag, had no intention whatso-ever of letting a load of Argentine military adventurers keep the Falkland Islands. She said, in her usual clarion clear tones, that the islands must either be returned quickly to Britain within a political settlement, or they would be taken back. The Argentine military junta said they were there to stay. They thought they were well dug in and safe. Unfortunately, the ordinary Argentine military were a rather simple-minded, stupid folk, who preferred to believe their own government's version of events. This was that the Kelpers were delighted to be relieved of the yoke of British domination, and that the islands were impenetrably defended by indomitable Argentine armed forces. Personally, I thought Mandla had a better understanding of the real situation than did the Argentines, but then, I am a little biased. However, that left me with a problem. I really think that all life, even an Argentine military life, is precious. (Yes, even Golden Balls' life.) Here were a load of idiots so thoroughly brainwashed by their own leaders that they genuinely believed that the retaking of the islands was politically and militarily impossible. I could see that there could be no possible political solution with these fools in the Junta in charge, and that a major military confrontation was inevitable. What should I do?

I was in a very privileged position, in that I ran the civilian medical services, which were heavily used by the invaders. I met their senior officers on a regular basis. I took every opportunity I could to ask them to consider the possibility, just the theoretical possibility, of the retaking of the islands by the British Task Force then being assembled and dispatched. Most of them laughed me to scorn. It was impossible. They really seemed to believe that. I kept trying. Eventually one particular Argentine air force commander did just begin to dare to think. What I asked for was a tented field hospital to be set up on the football field that lay between the hospital and Government House. Our hospital and their field hospital could then work together to care for the inevitable casualties of the forthcoming conflict. He made some enquiries of the Argentine army. Yes, at least in theory, they did have such an organisation. A five to six hundred-bedded air transportable field military hospital. Could he arrange to get it set up? He was posted away. He had actually dared to contemplate failure, and was disgraced. When I met these Argentine officers I usually took the opportunity to remind them that Britain was a nuclear power, and that their wives and children were all in undefended homes in the Argentine. Some, the less stupid, quite reasonably said that Britain would never do that. It would be immoral. So I asked them what the Argentine junta would do, if the situation were reversed. They were visibly shaken by this thought, and looked sick. It did not make me over-popular with the Argentines, but at least it made them think a little about the British Task Force, and what was to come. The Argentines actually distributed pre-prepared postcards of a pretty little white girl, aged about ten years, welcoming the brave Argentine invaders. She was meant to be a Kelper. It was regarded as being in very bad taste by the Kelpers, but it was really rather funny.

The three thousand Argentine regular commandos who invaded the islands were quite quickly replaced by three or four times that number of ordinary conscripts. They were mostly young, some as young as sixteen, but largely seventeen-year-olds. They were mostly from very poor peasant stock, presumably those who could not afford to buy their way out. They were largely from the much warmer North of the Argentine, which approaches a sub-tropical climate. They were in uniform and boots suited to a warm climate. A small part of the Argentine is actually south of the Tropic of Capricorn. The only item of warm clothing that many of them had was a sort of olive green anorak. They quickly became known as greenfly, and were referred to as such by the Kelpers on the radio. Several of the expatriate wives in Stanley felt really sorry for these young conscripts. Many had been recruited directly from poor country schools in the warm north of the Argentine, being told that they were going on a very grand mission that would make them national heroes for evermore. They had all heard of the islands, but had no idea that they were nearer to the South Pole than to the equator, both in position and in climate, and they froze in their light clothing. We do not know how many Argentines died in that war. The Argentines claimed to have lost under one thousand dead, which may be true of the actual battle casualties. However, both unofficial Argentine sources and unofficial British intelligence reports put the figure at between three and four thousand. The huge majority of these died not from acts of war, but from simple cold, hunger and exposure, because the Argentine logistic organisations were too incompetent to bring supplies of food, fuel and shelter to where the young soldiers needed them.

Mandla the cat kept himself well supplied throughout the war, stealing from Argentine and Kelper alike. He stole an entire custard pie from the librarian's kitchen. When the conflict was all over, he returned home a full, fat fur-ball.

CHAPTER 27

In between times

I WAS EXTREMELY concerned that if the Argentines expelled Dick Baker, the Deputy Governor, there would be no serious residual British authority left on the Falkland Islands. Things were obviously going to have to be done, and to happen, every day over the following weeks until the battle began to retake the islands. We knew, from the BBC World Service, that they were on the way, but it takes six weeks for a commercial ship to make the journey from Gravesend in Essex to Stanley, and to organise and train a fighting force would obviously take a lot longer still. Once the state of affairs was obvious, I called the remaining heads of department together. A few had accepted the Argentine offer to evacuate them and their families. Others, including myself, thought it our clear duty to remain with the severely traumatised islanders, and to try to minimise the loss of life during the retaking of the islands. We met quite openly in the hospital sitting room. The Argentines could see all the principals of the civilian administration making their way to the hospital at 4 p.m. each day. They did not try to stop us.

Our first priority was the physical safety of our people. The vet, Steve, and others, did a fine job of work, mapping out every stone or brick-built building in Stanley. Remember that the vast majority of buildings were of wood, with corrugated iron roofs. There were enough more sturdy buildings adequately scattered around Stanley to safely accommodate the entire remaining population of around 700 people. The normal population of Stanley was 1,000, but many had removed themselves to the Camp settlements for the duration of the occupation. We also set up a simple pyramid system of verbal communications. Each person would keep in regular, close contact with three or four other families, road by road, so anyone in trouble, from fire or injury, for example, could start a cascade message up the pyramid to get help, and information could be cascaded down the pyramid. People began to work hard and efficiently to help themselves and each other. The electricity station and central water supply were carefully maintained and functioned well. Tom, in charge of them, always did a great job. The Director of Public Works, Tom's manager, was away on leave. The library kept going, despite the efforts of our cat, Mandla. The hospital functioned tolerably well, despite Argentine conscripts stealing the wooden fencing from around the hospital gardens to light fires to keep warm. This could have let stray, hungry sheep wander in and eat all the patients' and residents' food. However, the conscripts ate the sheep as well, so a sort of balance was struck.

There were a few tense moments. Hilary was walking with the three children to our home, a mile away from the hospital where we were all staying. It was, for us, a bright, sunny, autumn day. The children were in shorts and light shirts. Gwyn, our youngest, now aged four and a half, pointed to a group of conscripts, who were visibly cold and miserable, and called out that it seemed they thought it was a cold day, and the children laughed. The Argentines were not amused. On another occasion Tudor, now nine years old, noticed two Argentines trying to shoot a Logger duck at a range of about twenty yards. This is a beautiful, white, almost totally inedible bird. The duck was floating fearlessly in the harbour. They were using their rifles. The duck studiously ignored them. They missed again and again, to Tudor's obvious delight. He had often been with me on the twenty-five metre .22 rifle range, and he well knew the accuracy with which a rifle should be fired at that range. He has since become an accomplished shot himself. But again, the Argentines were not amused.

Perhaps the service that we valued most that was kept going in those 'in between' days was the primary school. Steve the vet kept up his work caring for all the animals around Stanley. He had a lovely young wife who taught. She and a few others reopened the primary school in their own homes. I forget her name now, but she loved and cared for all the children, and we were very grateful that our three had something to take their minds off the war. We told our children, in the greatest detail that we knew, exactly what was going on, and the likely consequences. The decision to stay on the islands, and not to accept the Argentine offer to run away, was actually taken by all five of us together. It was a terrible burden to share with such young children, and I still have pangs of guilt about it. But when we discussed the options as a whole family it became very clear that we all really wanted to stay with our friends and patients and colleagues, and that we also wanted to stay together as a family. The Baker family, that of the Deputy Governor, very kindly offered to take our children back with them to safety in Britain when they were expelled. But the five of us really wanted to stay together. In the end, eighteen years later, I am very glad that we did. Hilary and I would now be ashamed if we had run away like so many others, and the children, far from suffering from their remarkable experiences, appear to have gained great strength and character from them.

CHAPTER 28

Heads of Department Committee

THE SINGLE MOST serious project that the Heads of Department
Committee undertook was to ask for Red Cross protection for
the civilian population. Under the Geneva Conventions there is a
provision for a civilian population at risk of harm from armed conflict
to request a 'Protecting Power' to supervise the removal of civilians
to a place of safety. The total population of the islands was only 1,700
people. They could have been moved in their entirety in one or two
ships to, say, Bolivia or Chile. I composed a message to the Foreign
Office requesting this. The Committee redrafted the message several
times, until all were satisfied with it. Our hospital secretary typed out
six copies. We kept one, and individuals returning to Britain took the
other five. At least two copies got through to the Foreign Office, and
another to the press. We were absolutely delighted to hear it read out
verbatim over the BBC World Service. It was signed by every Head
of Department remaining on the island, and by Mr Monk, the senior
elected councillor. Nothing came of it. Apparently the British
Government did not want an evacuation of the civilians, as this would
have reduced the reason for retaking the islands. The Argentines,
although we did not know it at the time, were not signatory to the
Conventions. (Only countries with a hint of civilisation have signed
them.) The Red Cross were lackadaisical about it all to put it kindly.
Eventually two Red Cross officials turned up, and talked to a few
Argentine officials, who reassured them that there was nothing to
worry about. There would be no conflict, no retaking of the islands.

It was a tense time. One afternoon an Argentine lieutenant colonel
engineer officer came in to see me at the hospital. He told me to
order the hospital cook, whom we later learned was an Argentine
collaborator, to prepare food for him and some of his officers. I told
him that this was totally out of the question as, under the Geneva
Conventions, a medical unit, even a military medical unit, must have
nothing whatsoever to do with supporting fighting units by feeding
them, transporting weapons for them, or the like. If they do, they
automatically and immediately lose all rights to the protection of the

sign of the red cross. He blazed with fury. He then collected himself together, and told me coldly that he knew how to deal with people like me, and I would soon find out. I held my ground, but it was the first time in my life that I have actually been sick with fear. That kind of vomit tastes revolting.

The day before our friend and neighbour, Dick Baker, was expelled from the islands, I was summoned to the Secretariat, where the Argentines had ensconced themselves. I was taken to the 'Deputy Argentine Military Governor' who was standing with Dick Baker and Hector the spy. He told me my exact salary and benefits – about £12,000 per annum. Not bad in 1982. He had it down to the last penny. He offered there and then, if I agreed to work for the Argentines, to triple my salary. I laughed politely and reminded him of the rate of inflation in the Argentine, about 80 per cent each year, and explained his offer was a bit of a joke. He could see that. Then I reminded him of a piece of paper on my hospital office wall that he had not liked seeing on a previous visit there. My Royal Commission. I told him that I had sworn allegiance to the Queen, and that I bloody well meant to uphold my oath. I continued by explaining that the Argentine invasion of the Falkland Islands was illegal and immoral. He was not best pleased. Dick Baker kept a perfectly straight face through all this. He was kind enough to congratulate me on my stance when we met later that day, but I think the Argentines did find me a little difficult.

We continued our radio clinics with each Camp settlement every morning. There were more people in the distant settlements than previously, swelled by the flight from Stanley, and they needed medical care and contact as never before, so every morning I walked up to the radio shack and talked to each settlement in turn. Eileen Vidal tuned and monitored the radio equipment as she had always done.

Now, I knew that the Royal Navy Icebreaker, HMS *Endurance*, always monitored the Falkland Islands Radio Service. Their officers had joked with me about our radio clinics, and how much more gentle Hilary was than myself on the radio. True. So I gave every settlement time enough to let me know whether they had greenfly (Argentines) or not, and whether there were any problems with 'scrap metal' (military installations). We built up over the airwaves a fairly detailed picture of the numbers, and the disposition of the enemy forces around the islands, and all this was carefully recorded and analysed aboard HMS *Endurance*. What a pity I despised the captain of that ship so deeply. It was a risky thing to do, but I judged it worth the risk if it could save the lives of our servicemen coming to rescue us. In retrospect, I have learned that the information was useful, but only to a limited extent. The real, hard information was needed several weeks later, when our troops were actually about to land. By then we had Special Boat Service (SBS of the Royal Marines) ashore, giving up-to-the-minute accurate information.

CHAPTER 29

The Church

A S I SIT HERE, 2,000 feet above the Mediterranean Sea, on a beautiful moonlit evening, I wonder if it all really happened. The moon is one day past the first quarter, and is very bright, with a beautifully pure silvery light. The only sound I can hear is the occasional call of a frog. The world appears at peace. Hilary is reading a novel close by me. Then I remember the violent history of this place. Yes, sadly, it did all happen. So on we go.

At the time of the invasion I was a deacon of the Church of England. I preached regularly at Stanley Cathedral, and took all the services when Harry Bagnall, the chaplain, was away in the Camp or on leave. We, Harry and I, were not getting on too well. He was rather evangelical, and I am more middle of the road in my churchmanship. He loathed the military, and I am steeped in them and in our traditions. He was appointed 'Visitor' to my hospital, or, more honestly put, an inspector. The matron, Jackie Gant, did not get on over well with Hilary and myself but she got on a treat with Harry. She was on leave in Britain when the Argentines invaded the islands. The Bishop of the Argentine, one Robert Cutts, had been to visit us before his fellow countrymen invaded us. A man of English origin, he came to a meal in our house. We mentioned that our previous tour had been in Swaziland and that the Bishop of Swaziland had made me deacon there. Bishop Cutts said, 'What a sad people. They do not even have the word "Thank you" in their language. Poor savages.' We were incensed. Technically, he was right. It is not a word in SiSwati; it is a gesture, a raising of one hand held by the other, a movement far more powerful than a word. They do actually have a word, *siyabonga* (we praise you), but not a strict translation of 'thank you.' I dismissed my local bishop in my own mind as a semi-educated, arrogant man – a true representative of the Argentines.

So, with this rather sad and confrontational relationship with my local church, into which I had been baptised, confirmed, and made deacon, I was in deep need of spiritual strength and sustenance. The invasion was on a Friday morning. On Sunday, 4 April 1982, we

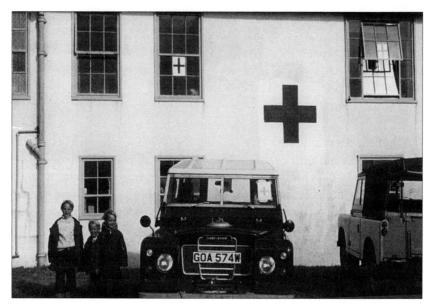

The children in front of the hospital. Mid-April, 1982.

'celebrated' Easter Day. Dear old Harry, (not Old Harry!) did his best. He took for his text the reading from the prophet Jeremiah, where he is addressing the Jews held captive in misery in Babylon. In the passage he tells them to get on with life as best they can, to build houses, to grow food, to have sex and reproduce, and to serve the Babylonians quietly, so that eventually their successors could return to Israel. Was Harry actually telling us to carry on as normal under the Argentines? He has since died, and I shall say little more about him. That same Easter Sunday our Roman Catholic colleague took a series of masses in their little church. They were packed with Argentines. The Argentine soldiers were told to leave their rifles outside the nave in the porch of the church. Later on Monsignor Spraggon told me how upset he had been on seeing so many pictures of the Blessed Virgin Mary glued onto the butts of those rifles. He and his priest, Daniel Moynihan, had a hard theological time, but they had real courage, as I shall show later. For myself and for my family our Christian faith was our strength and our salvation. It was of a practical, working type but it was real and it was effective. At the end of each day, including the day of the invasion, we met together in our communal bedroom. We talked about what had happened that day and Hilary and I told each other, and the children, all the news we had. Each of the three children had time to talk and to ask questions, often difficult questions. When we were ready we would say the Lord's Prayer together, a thank you prayer ('Thank you for the world so sweet, thank you for the food we eat . . .'), an asking prayer ('Through the night the Angels keep: watch beside me when I sleep . . .'), and the evening collect ('Lighten our darkness, we beseech you, O Lord . . .'). Then each of us would pray as we wished. I remember Catherine asking for our safety and our survival. Then I would end with the blessing. This pattern continued right through the war. It allowed each of us to bring our hopes and fears before God. It allowed each of the young children to bring their own joys and terrors into focus, and to be able to share them with us. Personally, I find the saying 'The family that prays together stays together' trite and horrible. But I cannot deny it.

After that Argentine Lt. Colonel engineer made me throw up my lunch, a taste I shall never forget, I actually managed to steady and compose myself by saying, carefully, phrase by phrase, the Lord's Prayer. 'Forgive us our trespasses, as we forgive them that trespass against us . . .' Perhaps I learned to use that prayer as a tool, as a weapon, to control myself and my anger, but never to perfection. I was not able, and I still struggle, to regard the Argentines as fully human. I know, in my logical thinking, that they must be. I am very happy with every other race and people that I live and work with and I know that forgiveness is essential to my own salvation. But it is hard, very hard. God alone knows what our parents had to forgive after the Second World War, or the people of the remnants of Yugoslavia do today. Time does help, but it is a hard and humiliating process.

CHAPTER 30

The Taskforce is coming

THE HOSPITAL COOK upset me. General Galtieri, the Dictator of the
Argentine, made a morale-rallying flying visit to the islands. The
cook prepared a fine meal for him in the hospital kitchens. She was
of Argentine origin herself but I regard her as a collaborator. It was a
foul and filthy act. If the savages had been signatory to the Geneva
Conventions then her action would have compromised our protection
as a medically-privileged place.

We had painted huge red crosses on the hospital roof, clearly visible
from a mile away. They later made a good, clearly visible landmark
for our pilots. The largest was even visible from a United States spy
satellite passing overhead. It was a good move that Steve, the vet, had
thought of. We had two cars, a Land-Rover and a Mini, so that Hilary
and I could work and move independently in more normal
circumstances. The long-wheelbase Land-Rover was useful for any
travel off the roads, which only existed in Stanley, and was ideal for
camping trips. When the Argentines invaded, we put the Mini away
in a garage. We also packed up most of our belongings in crates in
the garages, so that they would be less likely to be damaged by
Argentine looting, or by bullets or fire during the reinvasion. Our
garage was constructed of breeze blocks, our house was made of
wood. For seventeen days after the invasion we were kept very busy
indeed, as was everybody else, both in keeping all the normal,
necessary activities going, and with making what preparations we
could for the retaking of the islands.

Tension heightened noticeably when Britain declared a two-
hundred mile exclusion zone around the islands. All Royal Navy
submarine movements are necessarily kept secret, but the common
presumption was that one was around. Nuclear submarines can travel
at great speed, and one may well have been sent before the Argentines
actually invaded the islands, while they were mucking about on South
Georgia. It may all become public knowledge thirty or fifty years after
the event, but even now very little has been released to the public on
our submarine movements during the Second World War. Whatever,

the Argentines became very edgy, and their 'navy' became very cautious. Their aircraft, especially their Hercules and their Pucaras, continued to fly a lot. A Hercules is a large military transport aircraft that can take off and land on a very short and rough runway. Being very robust, they serve the military of many nations very well. The runway at Stanley airport was ample for them, even fully loaded with troops and supplies. The Pucara is a locally-made twin-engine fighter aircraft, able to fly quite slowly. It was well-armed with machine guns. They found it ideal for killing their own people in punishment raids whenever there had been civil unrest in their miserable country. There is now a fine specimen outside the main entrance of the Army Air Corps museum at Middle Wallop. This was a spoil of war, and we all rejoiced to see it loaded onto the deck of the supply ship *Atlantic Causeway* when the war was over. Well worth a visit.

The Argentines also had a small, heavily armed coastal patrol boat, in which they proudly motored round and round the inner harbour at Stanley. I have no idea what they usually used it for. Shooting up recalcitrant fishermen, perhaps? They started searching people's houses again, looking for arms and ammunition. We got a very thorough going-over. They knew I was a marksman in the Army, and a regular member of the local rifle club. All they found in our house was an Army Blues uniform, which is an elaborate Army uniform for ceremonial parades, not quite the stuff of war.

The Argentines were also very worried about some missing Royal Navy seamen. They had been busy making sea charts of the coasts around the islands, charting depths and obstructions to shipping. A more peaceful occupation would be hard to find, so too a more gentle group of sailors. However, the Argentines were convinced that they were deadly and dangerous, and that they must be being supported by the Kelpers, so they kept on and on searching the houses. It appears that this group of Naval cartographers were so ensconced in their work, on one of the many very remote coastlines, that they had not realised that the islands had been invaded. Once they did find out, they gave themselves up, and were promptly expelled back to Britain.

Little by little the Argentines began to hear things that they did not wish to hear. All the residents on the islands listened carefully to BBC World Service. It was also rebroadcast by Falklands Radio. The BBC then also laid on a special programme for the Falkland Islands, and for the approaching Naval Task Force. No details were spared of the numbers, the airpower, the firepower, and the sheer might of the coming force. The Argentine propaganda machine, meanwhile, kept on and on telling their conscripts that the retaking of the islands by a country so far away was quite impossible. When Stanley Airport was bombed they began to realise something of the truth, and they got really nasty.

The Argentine military governor, General Menendez, kept issuing edicts. The first said that he was in charge of the islands, and that his word was law. Another ordered us all to drive on the right. As Kelpers had driven on the left since time immemorial, and all the road signs and markings were for driving on the left, this made our icy roads really hazardous. Another edict said that we must all respect the Argentine flag that was flying in several prominent positions. Some unruly Kelper youth pointed them out and laughed at them. They were badly beaten up for their efforts.

CHAPTER 31

Abduction

ON THE SEVENTEENTH day after the Argentine invasion of the Falkland Islands they came for us. Two officers waving pistols and two conscripts. They were clear and direct. 'Pack all you need in two suitcases, and come with us. You have got ten minutes.' I asked why, and where to, and was told I was wasting the precious ten minutes allowed. They were clearly very experienced at their job. I remembered the engineer lieutenant colonel. I remembered Major Dowling. I remembered that the Argentines 'disappeared' two thousand of their own people every year, for not agreeing with their savage dictatorship. There was nothing I could do but tell Hilary and the children, and obey.

By pure good fortune we had brought everything we needed to live, clothes, radio, children's favourite toys and books, to the hospital. We had virtually shut down our house, expecting it to be severely damaged in the retaking of the islands. Our idea was to bunker down in the safest, breeze-block-built section of the hospital, and do what we could from there. So we did pack into two suitcases, in less than ten minutes, under the watchful eyes of the enemy. We were then hustled out, two adults and three young children, down and into the front of the hospital, and into our own Land-Rover. The Argentines stood around for a few minutes, looking at their watches. Then one of the pistol-toting officers got in immediately behind me. I was told to drive to the police station, which was very close to the Roman Catholic church. There was a small group of people outside the church, and I stopped and told them what was happening. Someone said that Gerald Cheek had also been taken away. He had no idea what was happening. Gerald Cheek was Director of Civil Aviation, a Falkland Islander, intelligent, educated, and deeply committed to the safety of the Government Air Service. He was a striking ginger redhead, with a pleasant and hard-working wife. The soldiers had got out of the Land-Rover and one had gone into the police station. The group of people around us melted away. Wise thinking. Hilary saw Harry Bagnall, the Anglican priest, driving towards us in his Land-Rover. She waved to him to stop, and climbed out of the back of our car to brief him, and to try to get him to intervene. One of the officers came between Harry and Hilary, and said, 'Keep back, or I'll shoot you.' Harry retreated. At that moment Hilary noticed a movement of magenta and black at the church door. It was Monsignor Spraggon. He looked around as he prepared to descend the church steps and saw the tense little group at the back of our Land-Rover. He hurried down, calling, 'Hilary, what is the matter? Are you all right?' Again the Argentine bully started waving his pistol. 'Come any closer, and I'll shoot you!' Monsignor was made of sterner stuff than Harry and, not slowing his pace at all, he said to the officer, 'My son, if shooting an old priest is going to help you, you had better get on with it.' He then embraced Hilary, who gave him a brief résumé of the situation. He promised to help. We later learnt that he and Harry went off together to see Menendez, the Argentine-appointed military dictator/governor, to get assurances of our safety.

We drove the two miles on to the airport, built on a peninsula joined to East Falkland by a narrow strip of sand-dunes. We were told to go to wait in the arrivals and departures building, a single room served as both, inside a small building. There were several other individuals and another family there, some more frightened than us. A Kelper, Mr Wallace, with his young part-Argentine wife, three-year-old daughter, and nine-month-old baby son, were the most distraught. I suppose they knew more about Argentine behaviour at that time than the rest of us. Mr Wallace was Director of the Cable and Wireless office, which handled all telecommunications with the outside world in normal times. Another of his staff had also been arrested. Gerald Cheek was there. Velma, leader of the Girl Guides, and also an ace shot in the rifle club, was there with her husband, so there were thirteen of us, under guard, in the tiny airport lounge. The tension was terrible. The Anglo-Argentine asked several people around what was going on, and what was to happen to us. He was told to shut up. Then I spotted an officer looking at me in a surprised and curious way. He was a lieutenant colonel in the dental branch of the Argentine medical service, and had accepted and respected the principle of working with us under the terms of the Geneva Conventions in our hospital. Robert Watson, our dental surgeon, and I treated Argentines with dental problems in just the same way as we treated our own people, and this officer had helped us out whenever he could. He was senior to all our guards. He asked me what we were doing there. I asked him the same question. He looked very surprised, and went off to talk to some other officers. On his return he told me that we were all considered to be dangerous and subversive people, and several senior Argentines wanted us all to come to some considerable harm. Therefore, for our own safety, we were to be flown away to a distant settlement, somewhere in the Falkland Islands, but he did not know where. A strange explanation, but there it was. We were all boarded on a Puma helicopter, and flown over East Falkland, over the Falkland Sound, and on to West Falkland, to land at Fox Bay East.

CHAPTER 32

Arrival at Fox Bay

WE LANDED AT Fox Bay East, a part of the second-largest settlement outside Stanley. Combined with Fox Bay West, Fox Bay normally boasted a population of nearly a hundred people. It had the only landing strip for the Islander plane with an actual fire tender. This was a splendidly Heath Robinson contraption that could be towed along behind a Land-Rover. The only problem with the runway was that it had a major hump in the middle, so there was a tendency when landing in the Islander to touch down, be catapulted back into the air for a very brief flight, and then immediately to land again in a stall. Quite safe, but alarming. Unfortunately it bent the aircraft from time to time, which put it out of service for weeks at a time, whilst it was straightened out and then put through lengthy flight worthiness tests.

Our helicopter landed not at the airstrip, but rather right outside the Fox Bay East farm manager's front door. I do not know how he had upset the Argentines to be so treated, but he was bluntly told there and then that he had thirteen guests for an indefinite stay. He and his wife were ever so kind, and fixed a good solid meal of mutton and potatoes with fresh bread and butter, all home-made by themselves. They had two spare rooms, and we spent a little time debating whether to put all the men in the smaller room, and the women and children in the larger one. It was a great joy to be alive, and relatively safe, and not 'disappeared'. The manager of Fox Bay East conferred by telephone with the manager of Fox Bay West. They had a real telephone, that was connected by wires on telegraph poles. Some more remote settlements used the top two wires of their barbed wire fences to run the telephones, but much power and clarity was lost, especially after the all too frequent rain storms. The managers decided between them that it would be better for their 'guests' to be accommodated in the much larger house at Fox Bay West. Richard Cockwell, the manager at Fox Bay West, had struck up a reasonable relationship with the Argentine officer in charge of the garrison there. He was a reservist, and only worked part-time in the army. His real occupation was as an architect, and he was not quite as fanatical as the regular officers. So after our excellent meal we were all moved over to Fox Bay West, which was to be our prison until relief came from England.

The farmhouse was substantial, built of wood, with a corrugated iron roof, and two sturdy stone-built fire places. It had multiple small rooms. The Anglo-Argentine family of four, and our family, were each allocated a whole room. Luxury. Hilary and I had a substantial double bed, and we made a triple bed up on the floor, between us and the wall, protected by one of the stone-built fireplaces. Our bed springs were old, rusted, and very, very noisy. Whenever either of us turned over we were all woken by an orchestra of complaining springs. The bed in the room next door was the same, and the thin wooden walls acted like the sound box of a violin. We all learned to keep still at night. Sex was off the agenda. Someone once managed, further down the house, but all seventeen of us knew every detail of the performance, thanks to the sonorous bed springs. It never happened again in our seven weeks as prisoners there. Too embarrassing.

Richard and Grizelda Cockwell were very bright, keen and innovative sheep farmers. They had two very active young sons, so we had seven children altogether – Tudor, the oldest of all at nine and a half, and the nine-month-old Anglo-Argentine baby the youngest. There were ten adults. The Cockwells were fairly free to look after their farm. The rest of us were told very clearly that if we strayed from the immediate environs of the farmhouse, the conscripts had orders to shoot to kill. There was a high wooden paling fence around the house and garden. There was a large Argentine flag flying from a pole in the front garden. Since the edict that we must all show respect for their flag, and the Kelpers in Stanley being beaten for laughing at the stupid thing, we studiously ignored it.

The farmhouse had a fine series of vegetable gardens, peat sheds, cow sheds, chicken house and sheep pens. At first the Argentine officer was quite happy for us to use these large, allotment-like vegetable gardens as part of the 'immediate environs' of the house. The house was a hundred yards from the coast. An Argentine supply ship was very heavily, deliberately, beached on the coast, just opposite the house. The frightened crew had run it aground in what they hoped was a relatively safe place when they heard about the exclusion zone, and British submarines. They were horrified to find that they had actually grounded their damned ship about two hundred yards from the Argentine headquarters organisation on West Falkland. Too late. There was no escape for them, for their ship really was grounded. They knew what was on their ship. I could only guess, and I underestimated by a factor of ten. I estimated that it would probably carry about five hundred tons of explosives and armaments. I later learnt that they had nearer five thousand tons of lethal shells and armaments. About a quarter of a mile inland, uphill from us, was an Argentine fuel dump. We, in our wood-built farmhouse prison, were between a rock and a hot place.

CHAPTER 33

The farmhouse

M Y THOUGHTS TURNED again to safety. Our little bedroom was protected on the seaward side by a stone-built fireplace and chimney in the room across the passage outside. I decided it was as safe a place to sleep as any in the house. There was immediate, easy access to the back door, via the kitchen and pantry. Outside was a large peat shed that could be used if bullets were flying. If the back of the house caught fire, we could escape easily through the front. The wooden house was a sort of extended bungalow, all on one floor. I spent two days reorganising the peat blocks in the peat shed to leave a safe, protected area in the middle. Peat blocks are about one foot cube, very heavy, and extremely fibrous. They burn slowly and well, but being so fibrous they make an excellent shield against bullets and shrapnel. Each fibre slows up the missile, so it rapidly comes to a complete stop. Even a modern, high-velocity bullet will stop after passing through only two or three blocks of peat.

I found the physical exercise therapeutic. I spent much of the next four weeks digging in the large vegetable gardens. It was late April and early May, so late autumn and early winter, and not a time for planting, but it was good to dig over and prepare the soil for spring. The well-stocked chicken shed was doing well, in full egg production. All organic waste, such as potato and carrot peelings, were carefully collected into a large tureen, and were boiled up and cooked to a chicken gourmet perfection every day. These were then allowed to cool and were taken to the chickens when about body temperature. This was called 'hot mash', and it encouraged good laying even on frosty and snowy days.

The storeroom was very well stocked with large sacks of flour, sugar and rice. There were just about adequate root crops from the gardens, but they had to be conserved sensibly. Velma's husband had been a professional baker, and made some excellent breads. Mutton was plentiful at first. Later on the Argentines pulled up all the wooden fences to burn in order to try to keep themselves warm. The sheep then had free range and seemed particularly happy in the minefields that the Argentines had laid. Not even the Argentines, brave and hungry as they were, dared to go after them. So we were reduced to Spam from the larder, an old Second World War favourite. The ladies organised a cooking rota, and each provided the very best they could from the limited ingredients available. I well remember Hilary making a batch of Welsh cakes, a sweet, spiced, scone-like cakelet, with sultanas in them. They were very well received, but alas the spices were in short supply. The men devised complicated ball games and we developed a jogging track around the house, within the perimeter wall. We tried to keep as fit as we could. We also devised ball games and running and jumping games for the children. These games had to accommodate a three-year-old, a nine-year-old, and everyone in between, so we devised complicated handicaps. Only one window got broken. It all kept us fit and busy.

Back to safety. We painted 'Civilians. British' in large red letters on the side of the house and on the roof. Every few days Harrier jump jets flew very low over us. They would either machine-gun the Argentine headquarters that was very near to us, or drop bombs on Argentine arms dumps. We were very keen that they didn't bomb us, shoot us up, or set the nearby fuel dump alight. Had they hit the grounded Argentine supply ship it would have been a very swift end for all of us. We noticed that about two hours after every raid they flew over us again, following the same route as each raid. We correctly surmised that these second flights were to photograph the damage from each bombing or shooting raid. They did in fact identify our house correctly, and never hit us. But not from our writing 'Civilian. British.' We set up something far more easy to photograph from the air. There was a long washing-line, with a right-angle bend in the middle, set up in the paddock behind the house. The ladies hung up a large number of adult and of small children's clothes, to emphasise the difference in sizes. They also hung up every spare bra and pair of knickers that they had. Some were quite frilly and pretty and it made a magnificent sight. We had just got all this set up, to my complete strategic and aesthetic satisfaction. I was sitting on an oil drum, whilst Hilary was cutting my hair. She acquired this skill during our various previous travels, and useful it was in the Falkland Islands, where there were no professional barbers, only sheepshearers. So there I was, like a contented sheep, when there was a thunderous blast of two Harrier jet aircraft immediately overhead. They fly so fast, and so low, that you cannot hear them until they are actually over you. Scary.

Just before they had passed overhead, each had loosed two five-hundred pound bombs. Bombs have to be released well before the aircraft is actually over the target, because of their continuing rapid forward movement. Otherwise they would, of course, overshoot the mark. These Harriers were after an arms dump over the hill. So two Harriers and four large high-explosive bombs flew fast and low over my partially completed haircut. We made a dash for our children, and for cover. Four almost simultaneous explosions rocked the ground like an earthquake. It took us some time to find the valuable haircutting scissors again, before Hilary could complete the job. Sure enough, the Harriers reappeared a couple of hours later to photograph the damage – to the arms dump, that is, not to the dignity and repose of my haircut. We later heard that they got very precise, clear photographs of the children's clothes and the ladies' undies, and they correctly identified us and our position.

CHAPTER 34

Living in captivity

ALL THE AIR RAIDS were extremely exciting. They were so sudden, and so dramatic, that they seemed to be over before they had started. Our wonderful captors developed an early-warning system. As soon as intelligence came in that a raid was on the way, they would start shouting to each other 'Allerto! Allerto!' We never heard this alarm before a raid, only after them. I enjoyed the machine-gunning raids the best. The pilots would take a fix on our house, and then fly very, very low, just on either side of it, gunning down Argentine communications equipment, and anything else of a military nature that they saw. As far as I know, they never hit a soldier.

One day, as winter was advancing, the ground was iced over after a few days of frost. The ground became too hard with frost and ice to dig at all. We used a pickaxe to collect some potatoes. There was a dusting of snow blowing around in the brilliant, icy cold sunshine. A good flying day. An Argentine had a forty-gallon drum of drinking water in a wheelbarrow, taking it towards their cook-house. He had a shovel and a rifle slung behind his back and was struggling up the icy slope in front of the house, and we were all watching his slow progress with interest. Suddenly we heard the familiar roar of four huge Rolls-Royce jet engines. A split second later the Harriers were there, one on either side of the house, about fifty feet high, machine guns blazing. Of course, we could only see the one in front of the house, but we knew the other was there, from the blast of its engines and the rattle of its guns. Our hero with the water in the wheelbarrow froze for a moment. He had not been hit. The water drum, and the wheel of the barrow had. A flood of water flowed from the gaping hole in the drum, and the wheel disintegrated. The Argentine, in total panic, started to dig frantically at the ground with his trusty shovel, as if to dig himself a trench for shelter. The ice yielded not an inch. He eventually fell, exhausted and shocked, but totally unharmed. When we had recovered from our mirth at the event, we rushed outside to re-arrange the washing on the line, ready for the next aerial photography

16 May, 1982, my 39th birthday, taken from our bedroom window in our prison farmhouse.

session. Another dramatic shooting up was on 16 May, my 39th birthday. The Harriers gave me a scene to remember it by forever. They did their usual double fly-past. But on this occasion they hit the farm's aviation fuel supply shed, about fifty yards from the house. It made a magnificent birthday fire display, flames and black smoke rising to the heavens.

The accuracy and the intensity of these air gunning and bombing raids, and their skill at avoiding us, made the enemy intensely suspicious of us. They made regular searches of us, and of the prison farmhouse, looking to see how we were communicating with the Harrier pilots. They had already impounded the only farm radio transmitter, and all we had were ordinary radio receivers. However, my rather powerful radio receiver was immediately suspect, and was confiscated. Only an imbecile could mistake an ordinary radio receiver for a transmitter, but there we are. Fortunately, one of the men had kept his very adequate radio set in the bottom of his laundry bag, on the top of which he had cleverly left his most dirty and most smelly clothes. He was rightly proud of his weeks' old, stinking, rotting socks. They served us well. The Argentines could not stand it, and they never found that radio. So we had BBC World Service news right to the very end.

The air raids were, indeed, always accurate in shooting up the Argentine West Falkland headquarters, although this was moved frequently. We now know, but we did not know at the time, that Royal Marine Special Boat Service personnel had been, and were, giving our forces accurate information on the disposition of the enemy. The first direct taste of British armed power was felt when a Vulcan bomber, a huge delta-wing long-range bomber capable of delivering multiple nuclear bombs, flew over Stanley airport, and bombed it with an oblique line of heavy conventional bombs. This virtually halved its usable length. The Vulcan was fuelled for this vast journey from Ascension Island, thousands of miles away, by an incredibly intricate relay of Victor tanker aircraft, with a huge number of in-flight refuellings. Technically, it was an incredible feat, and it scared the local Argentines witless. They now knew that they could be hit anywhere, at any time. It unnerved them.

Despite these occasional excitements, the days were mainly long and boring. We had been used to a very busy and active lifestyle, with frequent long walks out into the beautiful countryside of fine hills, mountains, rushing brooks and rivers, and dramatic cliffs and sandy bays – very similar to the Scottish Highlands. There we were cooped up in the farmhouse, and any activity at all was a pleasure, because it helped to pass the time. I found a copy of Macaulay's *History of Europe*, a substantial tome. I had a good time reading it from cover to cover, and it kept my mind active and away from the war. We decided to take the children's education seriously. Hilary spent much time with them on writing and reading. I worked with their arithmetic, and others helped with other subjects. They were very good about this in general, and our three were well up to standard when we eventually got home to England. One of the younger children was a bit naughty. When our Gwyn, nearly five years old, was working hard to read a simple children's story, he blurted out, 'That's easy. I can read that story without the book.' The older children thought this was hilarious. Tudor rudely referred to him as 'The flying fart' after his habit of rushing around the house making a fart-like sound with his lips. The name stuck.

CHAPTER 35

Shells and death

THE ROYAL NAVY Sea Harrier pilots were splendid performers. I could not appreciate them more. But the warships were not to be outdone. Every fourth night we would get a shelling – forty or so heavy naval high-explosive shells, from their 4.5 inch guns. That is, the width of the gun barrel is four and a half inches. Big guns. There was a routine to this. First, the ship's Sea Lynx helicopter would come overhead sometime after nightfall. You could hear it, but not see it. It carried no lights. If, as I did, you knew your constellations well, you could pick out which stars were missing overhead, as the helicopter hovered between you and them. The Argentines never succeeded in locating one with their anti-aircraft guns.

Once the helicopter had had a good look at us on the ground (they had night vision aids, and thermal imaging), establishing where we were and where the Argentines were, the warship would fire a single, ranging round. This would be well away from us. The ship was out of sight, a few miles out to sea. Then, gradually, under direct control from the observing officer in the helicopter, they would train in on their first target for the night. Very occasionally a flare shell would be fired, which would illuminate the area brilliantly, sufficiently for photography to assess the damage done. The flare shell is a heavy metal case, about seven kilograms in weight, that explodes out a flare at a predetermined height. The released flare burns a brilliant silvery white for about a minute and is supported from a parachute as it burns. The whole effect is very pretty, as well as dramatic. As the Navy fired each shell there was a boom far out to sea. Then, about thirty seconds later there was a flash, followed shortly by a mighty crumping explosion as the shell exploded over, or on, its target. The ground would tremble a little, then there would be a contrasting silence, broken only by the sound of the helicopter overhead. This always sounded quieter after each explosion, because of the deafening effect of each shell. And then the next shell, and the next, and the next, until the Navy was satisfied with its work.

Shell casing damaged larder. The entry hole of the shell casing can be seen in the ceiling.

They only made one, minor mistake. That was to fire a flare shell a little low one night. The flare worked well enough, but the casing hit a rocky ridge at very high speed, and bounced up and over, to land vertically on the larder roof of our farmhouse. Seven kilograms of shell casing falling at about three hundred miles an hour went straight through the corrugated iron roof, through the ceiling, between a very large, full egg box, a fine, imported whole cheddar cheese, and a case of lager, through the floor, and down about three feet into the rocky rubble underneath the house. I was the only one awake at the time. I always stayed up to watch the shelling, to see what they were taking out. On this occasion I thought that a shell

Some of the children lined up in front of the farmhouse, with the shell casing between Tudor and Gwyn.

had gone astray, gone through the house, and failed to explode. I was very pleased to be proved wrong when the shell casing was dug out the next day.

We heard on BBC that the Argentine battle cruiser *Belgrano* had been sunk, and that the last futile efforts to negotiate a settlement of the conflict peacefully were failing. The Royal Navy scored a direct hit on the Argentine headquarters in Fox Bay. We were searched yet again, with more anger and Argentine frustration. They found nothing. Then a horrible thing happened.

Stanley was also being shelled regularly. A Special Boat Service commando patrol had reported, mistakenly, that all civilians had been evacuated out of the east of Stanley, the area where we and many of our friends lived. The Argentines had many heavy gun emplacements among the houses on the two roads running out to the east of Stanley, the coast road, and a small road behind it. They were shelled heavily, just as we were. Then, one night, a shell exploded on the Director of Education's home, next door but one to our house. Several people were gathered there, including the vet and his wife. She and two other residents were killed by the blast. We heard of the tragedy the

The Argentine supply ship.

next day on the World Service. Because our daughter Catherine was so fond of this lady, a teacher who had brought her and other hospital staff children some ribbons, lace and materials to make dolls' clothing, to keep them busy whilst there was no school, we decided not to tell the children. This was a mistake. By the end of the day the three children had decided among themselves that something awful had happened, and they came together to confront Hilary and myself, and to demand an explanation. It was the first time that we had not shared the whole truth with them, and they sensed it. We regretted our decision, and we gave them the exact casualty figures every day thereafter. We told them exactly what we knew of the teacher's death. The most worrying thing about that incident was that, after family prayers that night, Catherine asked, 'Father, are we going to die tonight?' It was the fourth night, and our pounding was due, and it came exactly on schedule.

It intrigues me to this day that our children did not suffer prolonged post-traumatic stress syndrome, or anything like it. To have been under regular heavy naval shelling every fourth night for weeks was no suitable upbringing for three young children. The worst hangover was at a fireworks display on the Thames the following November the fifth. Gwyn had fallen asleep in Hilary's arms. He woke up when a firework made a big bang, and shouted, 'The Argies are coming back!' He soon settled down, but we avoided fireworks for some years after that. They are all rather strong-willed young adults now, but whose children are not? We are very lucky.

CHAPTER 36

The retaking of the islands

BY THIS TIME the Argentines realised that we must have a radio set hidden somewhere, because we always had up-to-date news of the war from the BBC. They chose not to find it. The news we gave them was the only accurate news they could get. The frightful propaganda that their own authorities were putting out insisted that all was going well for them, and that there had been no Argentine losses on land at all. They knew how many were dying around Stanley, Fox Bay, and in the hills and mountains. We knew that at least a part of the British Task Force had landed. We knew of the Battle of Goose Green, that fifty-two paratroops had died, that Colonel Jones had died, and just how he had died, leading his men from the front, as was his way. When we told the Argentines this they actually laughed at us. No, they said. No senior officer ever leads his men from the front. That is for the juniors to do. I found that an interesting insight into their military thinking.

After that battle there were many tense days, when little appeared to be happening. The raid on Pebble Island was cheering news, when several of their Pucara aircraft were destroyed on the ground, along with other supplies. It gradually became clear to us that a massive, full invasion force had landed safely around San Carlos, over Falkland Sound from us. It appeared that the Goose Green assault had been in part a diversion, to take the Argentines' attention away from the serious business of getting massive forces to the East and the West of Stanley, where the major action was to be. The Second Parachute Regiment, having won their hard-fought battle at Goose Green, marched straight on to fight again at Stanley. We heard about the actions at Fitzroy and at Teal Inlet. A pincer movement was developing on Stanley – about three thousand of our troops closing in on about nine thousand of the enemy, who had had seven weeks to dig in and fortify their positions.

Then things really began to hot up. The BBC World Service began broadcasting almost non-stop about the war. The hills and the low mountains around Stanley were all in the news, the very hills on which we, as a family, went walking or fishing. It was getting really tense. More paratroops, and more Royal Marines, were killed. Ships of the Royal Navy, and of the Royal Fleet Auxiliary were hit, with disastrous loss of life and of equipment. The landing craft HMS *Sir Galahad* was hit, with terrible loss of the lives of Welsh Guards. Who was going to win? The BBC reported every life lost, every mishap, almost as it happened. But there were some good moments. The Argentine radio was repeatedly broadcasting the sinking of one of our aircraft carriers, HMS *Invincible*. It was lovely to hear Brian Hanrahan, whose voice we had come to know well, reporting for the BBC, saying, 'I don't know which ship called *Invincible* they think they have sunk. I am actually standing on HMS *Invincible* right now, and she is fine.' The Argentines actually referred to their own radio service as the lie machine. Then, on another occasion, they claimed to have shot down two of our Harriers. They sounded convincing, claiming to have captured one of the pilots. We knew in accurate detail how many of their aircraft had been destroyed. The successful raid on Pebble Island had wiped out several in one fell swoop. That embarrassed them. Then several of their jet fighter bombers, Super Etendards, were got, one by one, by our Harriers, and one or two by Sea Dart missiles fired from ships. So we were very pleased to hear, correctly reported by the BBC, that their pilots had to take off from their home bases, but to return to other bases after each raid, because their fellow pilots were becoming demoralised by their constant losses.

So we heard from the lie machine that that two Sea Harrier jump jets had been downed, and even details of one pilot's injuries. Nasty. Then we heard Robert Fox's own voice, live, to the world. 'Well, I am standing on the flight deck of this carrier. For obvious security reasons I cannot tell you how many aircraft took off this morning. But I can tell you that I counted them all out, and I counted them all back.' Not one had been lost. One did apparently have some cannon shell holes through the tail. Big deal.

Around June the fourteenth and fifteenth the tension became almost unbearable. The Twin Peaks, the Murrel River, Tumbledown, all places we could see from our own home in Stanley. What was happening? Could the ammunition and supplies last out? Our men were a very, very long way from home, and severely outnumbered. The enemy had had many weeks to dig in. A well-constructed trench, blasted out of the rocks with high explosive, would be well nigh-impenetrable. The final act had clearly begun, and seemed to go on forever. And our future depended on it.

Then a flash news broadcast, via Naval Headquarters in Fleetwood. 'White flags are reported to be flying all around Stanley.' Oh God!

CHAPTER 37

Surrender

THE NIGHT OF 14 June was rather tense for us. General Moore had accepted, in outline only, the Argentine surrender. They, however, wanted to save face. They wanted a 'negotiated settlement', not a total surrender. He was having none of it. They wanted to surrender in East Falkland only, and keep the West, where we were held. He would have none of that either. They wanted their officers to be allowed to keep their personal pistols, because many of the conscripts were quite ready to murder the officers if they could. He did allow this. So even by the next morning we were still waiting to hear whether the surrender would include us, or whether there was to be yet more fighting, this time to take Fox Bay, among other settlements, by force. A hopeful sign was that the shelling of Fox Bay, which by now had become a regular nightly exercise, did not take place that night. Something good was definitely happening, but the BBC had no firm news for us. The sun rose, bright and clear. The fine frost glistened in the light. The children woke and dressed, and we all started breakfast, still uncertain of our future.

There was a distant beat of helicopter rotors. A big one. A Sea King. We rushed out to the front of the house, and looked out over the sea, where the sound was coming from. It approached gradually, swerving from place to place, as if inviting someone to shoot at it. It was clearly marked 'Royal Navy', and was painted in Royal Navy dark blue. No shot was fired. It started to land a couple of hundred yards from us. Gerald Cheek and I ran to meet it. All I can remember is running fast, and the children streaming out behind us, like captive birds let out of a cage. As we ran, I realised that we were running along the exact track where the unfortunate Argentine with his wheelbarrow of water had been. The aerial machine gun had marked the frozen ground with a long trail of pock marks. Gerald ordered the children back a little, and signalled to the loadmaster a clear, safe area for them to land on. Another of the aircrew had a general purpose machine gun (GPMG) mounted in an open door, scanning the area for trouble. Two naval officers, in rather formal Royal Navy

The Royal Navy arrives to take the formal surrender of the Argentines on West Falkland.

uniforms, jumped down. They emptied their bulging pockets of sweets and small bars of chocolate, and threw them to the ecstatic children. We took them to the Argentine headquarters, one of the houses. They went in, and accepted the formal surrender of West Falkland. It really was all over. Having done that, they came over to the prison farmhouse. We all piled out onto the front lawn. They lowered the loathsome Argentine flag, and ran up the White Ensign, the flag of the British Royal Navy. We were back under British sovereignty again. The children thoroughly enjoyed the ceremony. We heard over the radio, from the BBC, that Stanley was a mess, with many buildings destroyed by the fighting, and many others deliberately defiled with Argentine faeces. Many booby traps had been left. It did not sound too good, but we did hear that the hospital was intact. We managed to get into the now-deserted Argentine headquarters. There were all our belongings that they had taken away from us. We got our super Grundig Satellit radio back. (It is here with me now, on top of Kantara mountain, in North Cyprus, as I write this. Perfect World Service reception!)

Because of all the damage in Stanley, we thought that we would be asked to stay in Fox Bay for some time. Falkland Islands Radio

General Moore's Gazelle with the Argentine supply ship beached behind it.

came on the air again, and advised those who were in the outside settlements in the Camp to stay there for the time being, until houses could be made safe, and water and electricity services repaired and reconnected. This seemed reasonable enough to us. We were very surprised, then, when General Moore turned up, looking fresh and bright as if he were on everyday military business, in his little Gazelle helicopter. (You can identify this machine from far off by the characteristic high-pitched whine of its engine, and the tail rotor is enclosed in a casing above the tail. Although it will carry four people, it feels very small, almost as if it is wrapped around you.) He wanted to see us all, and to see for himself that we were all right. He was really concerned for all those who had been taken prisoner by the Argentines. Some of the Kelpers had been treated very badly indeed by their captors. Having ascertained that we were all physically well, and not too badly mentally traumatised, he explained that he wanted to get all civilian services back up and running as soon as possible. Civil aviation, communications, medical services – the lot. And we were the people, held at Fox Bay West, that he wanted back at work most urgently. Would we go back immediately? Would we just! We were delighted. A Sea King helicopter turned up early next morning. We all piled in, our two suitcases per family carefully secured in the baggage area. The loadmaster asked Hilary to hold on to Gwyn tightly, as the main door was left open with a GPMG set up in it. Some Argentines apparently did not quite understand what a ceasefire meant. There was still sporadic shooting going on, especially in the mountains. We took off.

PART IV

CHAPTER 38

Back to Stanley

UP WE WENT, door fully open, giving us a panoramic view of
Falkland Sound, a beautiful channel of sea between East and
West Falkland. We had crossed it dozens of times on medical flights
in the Beaver or the Islander, on our scheduled Camp visits, and on
emergency medical calls. It was totally different on this flight. The
sound was full of warships. A dramatic sight. Then on, round the
south coast of East Falkland, heading for Stanley. We approached
Fitzroy Settlement. There was smoke on the horizon. The pilot took
us out to hover over the still-smoking *Sir Galahad*, the landing craft
where so many Welsh Guards had just lost their lives, or been terribly
injured. It was a sombre sight, and a strangely appropriate way to pay
our last respects to those fellow countrymen of Hilary's who had laid
down their lives for our freedom. The loadmasters, pilot and navigator
were visibly affected by the terrible sight. After a little time there we
rose up again, and went on to Stanley.

We landed on the football field, between the hospital and
Government House. We went straight to the hospital to see how
things were. Our little GP hospital had been taken over by 2 Field
Hospital, RAMC, and was being very rapidly expanded with tents
and equipment into a fifty-bedded military hospital. Just the sort of
thing that I had hoped the Argentines would do, but they had never
got around to it. Colonel Tam Cook, RAMC, the Commanding
Officer of the Field Hospital, shared my office with me. My secretary,
Shelley, had left Stanley, and he took over her large desk. Together,
we set about developing this new facility, with combined civilian and
military staff and patients. I felt very comfortable and at home with
the RAMC. My own commission was in the Royal Army Dental
Corps, but I had worked in several Medical Corps hospitals in the
past, and had actually been taught, as a medical student, by two of the
RAMC officers now there in the Field Hospital. Hilary got on
especially well with the RAMC pharmacists and radiologists. We had
an old friend and colleague as consultant anaesthetist. We had a really
good consultant dermatologist and two fully qualified military

Outside the hospital, the day we returned to Stanley.

surgeons. We were medically replete! Over the next few weeks we got every difficult and puzzling case from the previous two years a first-class consultant opinion. Pure luxury. The only things they were really hesitant about were general practice and maternity. These two areas are not the bread and butter of specialists in other areas of medicine, so we still had a little work to do. But our main work was in building up the hospital for serious surgical work. One of the British Antarctic Survey base doctors came to join us. He kindly agreed to cover us for a few weeks whilst we went home on leave to England. He got on well with the RAMC too.

There were some terrible jobs to do. The islands were littered with Argentine explosives, landmines and booby traps. There were accidents too. A sidewinder missile was accidentally released from an aircraft on the ground, and several guardsmen were very seriously injured. The paras and the marines were a little overenthusiastic at trying out some of the Argentine weapons, and we removed the odd bullet here and there from some unlikely parts of their anatomy.

The Argentines had left large areas of the islands, especially around Stanley, heavily landmined. Not all the minefields were marked. A few of their officers volunteered what information they could remember, and some rather crude sketch maps were taken from the

Argentines when they were searched at the surrender. Several Argentines were formed into groups to clear the mines around Stanley. This was dangerous work, with inevitable mistakes, explosions and injuries. I watched with horror as a group of them dug up the landmines planted right outside our home, between the road and the sea wall. We never let the children cross the road outside our house again. As well as physical injuries, the Argentines suffered a great deal of sickness as well. They were weakened by eleven weeks of exposure, cold, wet and hunger.

As a sort of final act of revenge the Argentines had squatted, en masse, in all the schoolrooms and the public buildings in Stanley and defecated on the floors. They then smeared the walls, and spread their faeces liberally around the place. (This is partly why I regarded them, and refer to them, as savages.) This brave act of defiance did their health no good at all, and in their weakened state many became seriously ill with diarrhoea and vomiting. They were, of course, very well looked after in our hospital. The dental state of many of the Argentines was quite appalling. We could not possibly undo years and years of dental neglect, but we did spend a lot of time extracting the rotten shells of teeth, much to the relief of their owners. (You cannot even enter the British Armed Services with neglected teeth, let alone serve with them.) So a busy time was had by all.

CHAPTER 39

Our home

ON OUR FIRST day back in Stanley it was quite clear that the hospital was in good shape and in good hands. Only one bullet had passed through the roof, leaving two neat little holes. I wanted to know what our house was like, but nobody could tell me. I walked the beautiful harbourside mile home that afternoon. The sea-front houses along my way appeared remarkably unscathed. A group of Argentine prisoners were removing great rolls of barbed wire, and landmines, from the front lawn of Government House, to my left. On the right the harbour was packed with more ships than I had realised it could hold – supply ships, fuel tankers, naval fighting ships, and two British Rail cross channel ferry boats. The five to ten yards wide strip of peaty land between the road and the harbour wall had little notices all along it saying 'Mines' in English. There were rolls and rolls of barbed wire there anyway. I walked on, past the war memorial, towards home. Just opposite the war memorial, which is on the sea side of the road, was an Argentine helicopter. It was the very one that had taken us, as prisoners, to Fox Bay. I was very pleased to see it there, well shot up. Later on the children almost danced around it. On I went, past our neighbour, Mr Buckett's house (he was the Government Transport Manager). His house appeared intact. On past our dividing hedge, and there was our own front gate, our own lawns, front vegetable garden and lovely house. All intact.

At the gate was a heavily armed sentry, with another just behind him. I glanced around, and saw others posted all round our house. There were piles of military equipment on the lawns. The hothouse had lost several windows, and was also full of military kit. There were little two-man tents up all over the lawns and paddocks. The second sentry accompanied me to my own front door. He called the Sergeant Major, who asked who I was and what my business was. I explained, a little surprised, that I was the doctor, and that I and my family lived in this house. His face fell, and he politely asked me to wait for a few minutes, in my own porch. A few of the panes of glass had been broken by shrapnel. He went up to get his Officer Commanding,

Major Jenner, OC 'C' Company of 2 Para, the Second Parachute Regiment. The Company pennant was flying proudly on my front lawn. Major Jenner came downstairs to meet me in the porch. He looked tired and strained. I later learned that he had a painful shrapnel wound, but he never mentioned it to me. He explained that his Company had been at, and around, our house when the ceasefire happened, and they had all been utterly exhausted. So he told them to take a break just where they were. He said that they would all be out of the house within two hours, but please could they use the garden and the outbuildings. He was very sorry for the inconvenience, but he hoped I would understand. He really, genuinely, meant this.

It was cold. There was frost at nights. Sleety rain fell in bursts, between some quite bright sunshine. He and his men had been out in the mountains in this for weeks, fighting for their lives, seeing some of their friends killed, and fighting for our freedom. I was appalled at the idea of telling fifty-seven exhausted men to go and camp in the snow in the garden. So we reached an agreement. They would clear one room, which had been Hilary's and my bedroom, and we would all five sleep in there. It was at least four times as large as our prison farmhouse bedroom. The paras could have the rest of the house. They were very pleased with this. There was no water, no electricity, and no food. There was plenty of heating oil in the tank, but without electricity to run the central heating, there was no heating. The house was horribly cold. Their cook, a true professional, had found our twenty odd chickens. He had fed them well with all the scraps left over from the Army meals of fifty-seven men. He had collected and used the eggs to supplement his cooking. The paras had unlimited supplies of food, liberated from the Argentines. The Argentines had stocked very many tons of food in huge containers in Stanley, but they had lacked the logistics and organisation to get it to their own troops in the mountains. There was an entire container, about forty tons, of best beef, all solidly frozen in the winter conditions. There were others full of so much pasta that they cooked extra for the chickens, in order to get more eggs. The garden was full of first-class greens.

Electricity was no problem to the paras. They asked for, and were issued, a brand-new 240 volt petrol-driven generator. This produced enough power to run the central heating pumps, power our wonderful radio, and run two low-wattage light bulbs. The central

The field kitchen. C Company, 2 Para, all fifty-seven of them, camped in our house and outbuildings for two weeks.

heating needed some repairs, but they called in the REME (Royal Electrical and Mechanical Engineers), and all was well. The house was warm and lit, and there was excellent radio reception. The men were so keen to hear the news from home that one man was left on duty listening to the radio at all times, in the kitchen, whilst doing any other necessary culinary duties.

Water was a problem. They transported in large containers of water which was rather dark and peaty, but made perfectly good tea and coffee, as long as it was made strong enough. They carried the water up to the cistern manually, and even got the bath going. Because of the difficulty of carrying the water, several took turns in the same bath full of hot water. They said it was fit to use as camouflage cream after the third or fourth man. They prepared a fresh bath for our family. So now we had the only house in Stanley with food, water, heating and electricity. I was so glad I had asked them to stay.

But far more than that was the feeling of security and safety. There were still odd shell shocked Argentines about, capable of any stupidity. When the paras had arrived and decided to rest in our house, they had searched it for booby traps. They found three – two hand grenades, pins pulled out, under upturned teacups, and a third wrapped in a tea towel. If Hilary, the children or I had picked up those cups, or that tea towel, it is most unlikely that we would have reacted in time to save ourselves. Hand grenades are solid, heavy metal bombs, and need a good deal of practice and training to be thrown safely. A child could never do it. Having armed guards all around the house in those first few days was an enormous comfort to us. There were odd explosions, day and night, from old mines going off, perhaps stepped on by sheep, and from the deliberate explosion of unsafe munitions. We were still in a rather nervous state, and having a crowd of professional soldiers around us was a great help.

The house was virtually undamaged. One piece of shrapnel had come in through Tudor's bedroom window but it did little damage in his room. Major Jenner searched for it, and found it embedded in a wall. He gave it to Tudor, who keeps it as a treasured souvenir, along with the cap badge given to him by one of the paras, and a precious red beret. The hothouse, greenhouse, and porch had all lost a lot of glass, but I was able to get some from Public Works, and a large tin of putty, and I patched them all up. Virtually all our belongings were safely packed up in the garages. The Mini was unhurt, and the Land-Rover was returned to us in excellent condition. We had been very, very fortunate.

Unlike our house, the police station was not left unscathed. Word had got back to the British forces retaking Stanley that Major Dowling had terrified and bullied many of the Kelpers left in Stanley, and that his office was the front room of the police station. They set up a rocket-propelled grenade launcher on the spit of land between the inner and outer harbours, facing his front window, and sent him a little present. This destroyed the office completely, but unfortunately he was not in it at the time. It did, however, help to remind the Argentines that they were very vulnerable to such attack, and was a help in encouraging them to surrender.

CHAPTER 40

Living with paratroops

OVER THE NEXT few weeks Hilary and I were very busy in the hospital. The schools were closed because both junior and senior school had been so thoroughly contaminated with faeces and were unfit to use. The Welsh Guards did a horrible, but very honourable, job in cleaning them up, disinfecting them, and making them fit for children again. But it all took time. This meant that our three children had little to do in the first two weeks back at Stanley. The paras in our house came to our aid. Many were fathers of young children themselves. Some felt pleased to be with the very children they had come to rescue from the Argentines. All were glad to have the warmth and shelter of our house. They took on our children all day, every day, for two weeks, until school reopened.

The paras were very pleased with a type of folding rifle that some Argentines had had. They chose a couple of hundred of the best of them, stripped them down, and cleaned them carefully. Our children became expert at this. They also found a large supply of Browning 9 mm automatic pistols, that had been the standard Argentine officer issue. These were lovingly cared for by the paras, and our children, and joined their armoury. They taught the youngest, Gwyn, how to wake up the sergeant major. He was well known to lash out violently in the first moment of wakening – a useful trait in a fighting para but a severe danger in normal society. Gwyn would first sing a line or two of 'Morning has broken, like the first morning, Blackbird has spoken like the first bird . . .' then stand well beyond the foot of his bed, lean carefully forward and wiggle his toes from this safe distance, standing well back in case his victim lashed out. It worked a treat, and this became one of Gwyn's regular chores.

The children were able to explain to the paras how everything in the house, the outhouses and the gardens worked. The cook was delighted with this. He had set up a very efficient field kitchen on our front lawn, immediately outside the kitchen door at the back of the house. There were three very powerful pressurised petrol field cookers, each capable of boiling two huge pots of water or food very fast. He was cooking for fifty-seven paras and three children, as well as for Hilary and me in the evenings and for breakfast. The food was basic, but very good and nutritious. The children told us gleefully all that they had eaten in our absence at work. They especially enjoyed the meals made partly from 'Compo' rations. Composite rations are made up in large cardboard boxes, containing a very well-balanced, nutritionally efficient, set of tins, enough to feed ten men for one day, or one man for ten days, or any such ratio in between. There are different boxes labelled A, B, C, and D, so that the menu can be varied through the week. They even include matches, sweets, tea, coffee, and toilet paper, so the troops using them only need a source of heat if the food is to be at its best, hot, and to make hot drinks, and a supply of drinking-quality water. All units carry water purification kits. The ends of the boxes are printed as targets, so are suitable for firing practice. The children loved them. We had three regular little paras by the end of the fortnight.

I managed to buy some cases of lager from Velma, who had been a prisoner with us at Fox Bay. She and her husband ran a small pub, but it was out of bounds to the paras. So we gave the lager to the paras. They, in turn, dined out our whole family one night, very formally. They took over one of the bombed-out houses behind ours, and lit it with pressure lamps. They curtained off the bombed-out windows and doors with tarpaulins and blankets. They cooked and served the most magnificent meal, with fine wines that they had found in Hector the Argentine Spy's house. It was an extraordinary, and a very memorable evening.

In the middle of this fortnight it came to snow heavily. As usual, there were intermittent bright sunny spells, when the whole country-side became dazzling white and very pretty. Between our house and Dick Baker's house was a small road running down at right angles to the harbour, about two hundred yards long and reasonably steep. I was very amused to find our children and the paras tobogganing down this slope of well-packed, icy snow at great speeds. No one ended up in either the minefield or in the harbour. There were no serious injuries at all.

One of the paras appeared to be the 'fall guy' for anything that went wrong. He always got the blame, and we wondered why. Brown appeared to be a really decent chap to us, but he could get nothing right with his fellow paras. Hilary took him to one side to find out more. The fact was that in the last terrible hours of fighting on the

Paras tobogganing.

mountain to the east of our house his glasses had come loose, and were smashed to pieces. He was very short-sighted, and desperately needed them for even the most basic of soldierly duties. Fortunately he had a note of his prescription. This is routinely issued with the standard service gas masks, in case they are damaged. Glasses cannot be worn inside a gas mask, as they would destroy the airtight seal between skin and mask, so they are made into an integral part of the mask. Laurence, the hospital secretary, was an expert at making up glasses from a standard set of lenses, as long as he had the prescription. The new glasses not only made an instant change for the better in Brown's social status, but it made a rough, tough set of paratroopers view Hilary in a new, almost mystical light.

Behind Dick Baker's house was the racecourse, a set of very rough turfy fields where I used to collect manure for my gardens, and we all collected mushrooms in the autumn. It was now the main military heliport, with helicopters coming and going at all hours. The Royal Air Force used the little road behind our back paddock as the main supply route to their helicopter airfield. We also used the same little road to get from the back of our house, over our paddock, to the main road. It became covered in a few feet of snow, drifted down from the mountain behind us. An RAF officer had left his Land-Rover parked carelessly, obstructing a part of the road that was still usable. Hilary, in our Land-Rover, tried to manoeuvre around this parked vehicle on her way home from the hospital, and slithered off the road and into the drainage ditch at the side. Being an experienced Land-Rover debogger, she promptly got out and started laying some old matting that we kept for that purpose in the back of the vehicle. This allows all four wheels to grip well, but it must be carefully placed in front of each wheel to be effective. So Hilary was busy with her matting, lying on her tummy under the back of the vehicle, in deep snow, getting it right. At this point a very posh RAF officer-type voice asked if he could be of any assistance. Rumour has it that the reply was not the most polite in declining his kind offer, and indeed, that he was offered some rather direct advice on parking his Land-Rover in future. Poor man. I know the feeling.

CHAPTER 41

Getting back to normal

TWO WEEKS AFTER our return to Stanley the Parachute Regiment were shipped back to Britain. Our house was suddenly empty but for us. Things quickly became shipshape again both at home and at school. School reopened, with much help and support from the Royal Army Education Corps (RAEC). As well as normal teaching, much time was initially spent on singing and acting. The children sang through and acted through the trauma they had all experienced. After a few weeks the children gave a magnificent performance of a pantomime, acting out how they had seen their war. Taught and aided by the Welsh Guards, they also gave a very moving concert. A huge amount of pent-up emotion was released in song and acting. Some was tense, some was funny. Argentines were represented as all wearing two left boots, or holding their rifles back to front. Welsh songs of loss and sorrow can expound grief in a most positive and healing way, and I believe this was a crucial part of the children being allowed to become children again. War scarred, certainly, having seen and heard things that no child should ever be exposed to, but allowed to return gradually to friendships, play, family love and school life. The Welsh Guards and the RAEC did a great job beside the remaining teachers.

The RAEC also set up a series of talks and demonstrations about landmines, bombs and grenades, and loaded weapons. These were scattered all over the islands. On our return home there were eight forty-gallon drums of napalm at the back of our paddock. Around the hospital were huge dumps of belts of machine-gun ammunition. Piles of bullets turned up in all sorts of unexpected places. Not all bombs and naval shells had exploded on impact, especially some that landed in soft peat. We were quite relieved when four-year-old Gwyn went out to play in the garden one day, and found a rifle in a tussock of tall, ornamental pampas grass in one corner of the cabbage patch. Remembering his school instructions, he called an adult, who called the duty Army officer. The rifle was fully loaded, with the safety catch off. Gwyn could have pulled the trigger quite easily. But he remembered his RAEC lessons. Good for them!

All the children of Stanley aged five to thirteen were invited to a huge party aboard the hospital ship, MV *Uganda*. This had been an educational cruise liner before being requisitioned for the war. It had functioned very well indeed. Not one single wounded soldier taken aboard alive failed to recover, despite many terrible injuries. But now the ship's duties were being taken over by our hospital. Catherine and Tudor went and had a wonderful time there, with all their school friends. Gwyn was just a month too young to be allowed to go – they were very strict about age because of the need to get up and down the gangways to and from the ship, which was moored out in the middle of the harbour. She was a very big ship, drawing far too much water to dock at the little jetty used by smaller ships. So Gwyn was invited, with Hilary, to visit the surviving supply ship, *Atlantic Causeway*. Her sister ship, the *Atlantic Conveyor*, had been sunk by an Argentine Exocet missile (manufactured and supplied by the French, thank you, France!) with near-catastrophic loss of our military hardware, especially Chinook helicopters. The seamen were delighted to see a child again. They had been away from their families at sea for months and Gwyn was terribly spoilt. He was loaded down with chocolate bars and souvenirs. On the main deck they saw the Argentine Pucara aircraft on its way to Britain to become a museum piece for the Army Air Corps. The little boat that took them out to this visit was the Argentine coastal patrol vessel, now owned by the Royal Navy, and renamed HMS *Tiger Bay*. There are centuries of tradition about capturing enemy warships as the spoils of war, and renaming them. This was no exception, but it does not happen often these days.

We had actually been due for mid-tour leave in May, 1982, when we were imprisoned by the Argentines. We were now well into July, and a passage was to be arranged for those who had been held captive, and others who wanted it. We did not know when it would be, but were asked to be packed up, ready to go at short notice when a passage could be arranged. We tried to get visits to Camp settlements back into a routine. Unfortunately both Beaver float planes and the Islander had been totally ruined in the battles around Stanley. The children and I went to visit them in their sheds. The planes that we had all enjoyed flying around the islands in so much were now sad wrecks riddled with bullet holes, and total write-offs. Our visit felt a bit like going to the funeral of a good friend. A whole way of life had been destroyed. We also drove out to the airport to see what the damage was there. It was a cold, snowy day, with a lot of snow and ice settled on a desolate scene of burnt-out and broken Pucaras, and Argentine helicopters. The main runway was damaged, but was under active repair. Hercules were able to land on it, but nothing requiring a full-length runway could do so. Whilst the runway was being repaired it could not even accommodate a Hercules. We heard that our first mail since the beginning of the war was about to arrive. It did, and we saw it coming. Two huge parachute loads of it, dropped out of the back of a Hercules, which had several refuellings both on the way out and the way back. What a service!

On either side of the road from Stanley to the airport were long areas marked off as minefields. In other places were mountainous piles of rusting Argentine rifles and other armaments. They had been taken from the Argentines as they had surrendered in their thousands, and passed through checkpoints on their way to a holding area on the airport peninsula. The weapons were doused in oil and petrol and set fire to, to prevent their use in the future. Everywhere we looked were signs of destruction and decay. 'Change and decay in all around I see, O Thou, who changest not . . .' So for our Camp visits we had to make use of what transport the forces' helicopters could provide.

Hilary was wanted for some medical work in Port Howard, on West Falkland. She was taken there in a Gazelle helicopter, pilot and navigator in front, and two seats behind. They had some difficulty accommodating her three bags of medical kit, but it was eventually stowed away safely, and the journey out was uneventful. Then the fog came down – nothing unusual, but they were stuck there. The message came that there was a passage home to England available for us the next day. The pilot was very kind, and promised to fly her home if he could safely do so. The next day was a little better, and they flew over the wave tops of the Sound to East Falkland, but were then lost for a while. The pilot hummed a high-pitched tune throughout. Then the navigator spotted the fence that runs up through a gap in the mountain range between the Sound and Stanley. He knew this route, and followed it safely homewards. They got back shortly before our boat was ready to leave. Relief all round. Then the Wessex pilot who was due to fly us out to the boat decided there was too much fog on the harbour. So we waited another day after all.

Our journey was to be in two parts; first a twelve-day sea voyage from Stanley to Ascension Island, about four thousand miles away, then an RAF flight to Brize Norton from there. We were lifted out

to our ship in batches by helicopter. Our ship was quite amazing. It
was the MV *St Edmund*, a British Rail ferry, normally used for the
Harwich to Hook of Holland route. It had the double arrow British
Rail logo painted large on the funnel. It had been requisitioned for
the war. The naval yard had built a huge helicopter landing pad,
supported on high girders, over and above the back of the ship at
about funnel height. It looked a bit odd, but it worked.

CHAPTER 42

The journey home

OUR JOURNEY BACK to Britain was a memorable adventure. The first twelve days were on the MV *St Edmund*. We were allocated a small interior cabin with two double bunks in it, and a very small space in between them – double bunks in the sense of one single bunk above another. So Tudor, Hilary and I had a bunk each, and Catherine and Gwyn shared one, feet to feet. There were six hundred Welsh Guards on board, of whose original number about fifty had been left behind, dead, at Fitzroy. There were also several hundred members of 3 Para, and about thirty civilians like us. As we set off from the inner harbour, through the outer harbour, and away from the kelp fields in the sea, I felt a strange sense of finality. The war really was over, and we were going home to see our parents and family again. My mother had had a stroke when she heard of our abduction. She was very fond of all her grandchildren, and feared for their lives. She lived another seven years, but never regained her full strength and mobility.

The waters around the Falkland Islands were still considered to be in severe danger of Argentine reprisal. Although they had surrendered, it was with ignominy, and they continued to lay claim to the islands. So we kept strict radio silence for the first six days, and spent the first three days on a wild zigzag course. Hilary being Welsh herself, and with sons called Tudor and Gwyn, we were very soon mingling and talking with the Welsh Guards. We were allowed to understand, and to share a little of, their grief at the loss of their friends and their comrades at arms. There were three forces chaplains aboard, and they were working at all hours, talking with the bereaved men. We had regular services of Holy Communion in one of the lounges. The first three days of our voyage were through very heavy seas. The waves of the South Atlantic can be huge, and our little British Rail ferry-boat heaved from side to side, and from front to back, both alarmingly and nauseatingly. The plates ground against each other with horrible metallic groaning noises. I just got through the first Communion service, and then had to rush to the heads

146

(toilets) to be sick. There, before me in the toilet bowl, was the Holy Sacrament that I had just received. What a theological dilemma! I let it go. Ashes to ashes, and dust to dust.

In the evenings we gathered at the lounge bar. At first we were limited to two cans of lager per person per night. They did not want any brawls between Welsh Guards and paras. Quite right too. That would have been very messy, by past experience. Later on this was relaxed, and the singing improved. Many of the Welsh Guards were superb soloists. They sang a rich variety of traditional songs, both in English and in Welsh. These were beautiful and deeply moving. They were of grief, of lost love, of faith, and of hope. There was also a Royal Marine band on board. They gave more formal concerts on the open deck when we moved away from the cold south, and toward the calmer, warmer waters as we neared Ascension. These were times to sit quietly, and to listen, and to ponder the last few months. At other times we just sat, and talked and talked and talked. There was so much mental baggage for all of us to unload, and those twelve days at sea gave us a chance to unwind among the best of people. Today I just hope that if any of my children go to war, they will have chaplains as good as we had aboard that boat. Music and song can be used in a stirring, nationalistic way. They can also be used in prayer, contemplation, healing and reconciliation.

After six days we were well out of Argentinian range. The days were longer, calmer and more sunny. The paras and the marines took over the upper car deck of the ferry as a gymnasium, and used the very back as a shooting range. They threw empty tins to float out behind the boat, in its wake, and practised their marksmanship from the back rail of the ferry, as soon as the tin bobbed up in the foaming water. When they hit the tin it would make a dramatic splash in the wake. Tudor compared this with the Argentines trying to shoot a logger duck. The lower car decks were full of the returning military vehicles and equipment. Radio telephones were established via a satellite connection. Half the press in England wanted to talk to us about our captivity. We did our best for them, but it is hard to tell a story like this in the short space available in a newspaper. A crewman found and inflated two children's paddling pools, and put them on the deck, full of seawater. The bright sunshine kept it pleasantly warm. The upper and the side decks now had sunbathing soldiers on them in abundance. Some started fishing over the side of the boat. Among other fish, they caught a number of very colourful piranha-like fish.

Our first, dawn, view of Ascension Island.

The children loved watching and feeding them in one of the paddling pools. They dared each other to play 'chicken' with their fingers. The fish had a very sharp bite. I only had to dress and bandage a few fingers.

Very early on the twelfth night, just before dawn, the ship's engines slowed down. This woke us at once. We all leapt up out of bed and went on deck. There, on the horizon, was the first light of dawn silhouetting the tips of the three highest of the volcanic mountains of Ascension Island. The island consists of about forty of these old, quiescent volcanoes, all conjoined, rising steep and sheer out of the ocean.

The island gets its name from being discovered on Ascension Day, many years ago. The tips of the mountains are over three thousand feet high, and are usually covered in a locally-formed cloud. The cloud moisture is collected in huge dew-pans, and it provides a supply of pure, clean drinking water for the inhabitants. These vast dew-pans, like the tunnels that have been dug through the soft volcanic rock to allow the water to go down to the villages, have all been dug and built by Royal Marines in years gone by. The mountain tops, being temperate in climate, are used as a large farm and market garden to supply the villages with meat, vegetables and milk. It is all very efficient and economical. The volcanic mountainsides are hot and exposed, with occasional brightly-coloured flowering shrubs growing in crevices. The beaches are tropical, covered in hot, black lava sand. We approached the scene slowly, in gradually increasing daylight. More and more of the mountaintops became visible. The colours of the sky changed from grey to a deep crimson red, and then gradually through a lightening series of reds and yellows to full daylight. It was incredibly beautiful, and peaceful.

CHAPTER 43

Ascension and home

A REPORTER FROM the BBC came aboard our ferry-boat whilst we were moored off Ascension Island for two days, awaiting a flight onwards to Britain, to get some stories. Whilst talking to me he learnt how valuable the BBC World Service had been to us, and how it kept us in contact with the outside world throughout our ordeal. He very kindly invited me ashore with him for a day, and then invited the whole family to visit on the day of our departure. For my day visit we hitched a lift on a helicopter both ways. There were plenty coming and going with post and supplies. I spent a fascinating day visiting the BBC relay station on the island. They constantly monitor the BBC from London for the clearest frequencies, which change according to the time of day and the weather. They then rebroadcast around the world with a freshly enhanced signal. It was the Ascension relay that we heard best in the Falkland Islands. I was also intrigued to see the small, but comprehensive medical facility.

When we finally left the *St Edmund* we were all picked up in a Chinook helicopter. The back was left wide open, so that we all had a magnificent view, first of the ocean around Ascension, and all the warships and supply ships moored around the island, and then of the island itself. There was no harbour, so all the ships had to anchor a little out to sea. Cargo and people had to be boarded and landed either by helicopter or by small boats. The pilot took us all around the sights of the island before landing at Wide Awake (the name of a local bird) Airport.

Once ashore, our BBC hosts took us to lunch in their home in the residential village halfway up the mountainside, where the air is fresh and pleasantly warm. The village is charmingly called Two Boats. It is really hot on the coast, especially after two years on the Falkland Islands. They then took us up to the mountaintop farm, and to the dew-pans, as large as fields, for a very welcome walk – our first hours off a little ferry-boat after twelve long, cramped-up days. The natural land up there was a sort of tropical dew forest, with a blaze of bright red amaryllis lilies on the ground. There were no landmines on

Happy ending. The children at Two Boats village, Ascension Island. Well, happy, and above all, alive!

Ascension, and the children could run wherever they wished. We have photographs of them playing hide and seek around some huge, exotically coloured bougainvillea bushes, looking ever so happy and relaxed. At the end of the day we went down to what had been one of the busiest airports in the world, despite its remote location. At the height of the war it had challenged Heathrow Airport for the numbers of flights daily. There were a huge mixture of transport, fighter, bomber and refuelling planes on the ground – a veritable plane spotters' paradise. We boarded an RAF VC10 for the journey back to Brize Norton, via Dakar, in Senegal. There was a military band playing when we got off the plane, welcoming the Welsh Guards with us back home. And then the press. And then our families. It was a whirlwind of excitement and emotion.

We never returned to the Falkland Islands. Golden Balls certainly did not want me back there, and who can blame him, poor little man. Tudor was ready to start secondary school, and all four of our parents were elderly, and had been through a mental hell not knowing what had happened to us. So we settled to a more conventional life in our home in London. Hilary went back into her previous discipline of community paediatrics, and is now a consultant paediatrician. Tudor joined the Royal Air Force, and is now a sergeant in a squadron, gadding about all over the world on various exercises and operations. I am a little jealous at times. Catherine and Gwyn both combined university with the Territorial Army. Catherine is studying midwifery, after two fine practical experiences of her own (we have two lovely granddaughters), and Gwyn went off to live on a houseboat in Cairo for a year to learn Arabic, and is now working hard in the Army himself. I returned to general medical practice in London, and did a little oral surgery, and have helped in managing some of the changes in British general practice. I have continued to have a very lively time in the Territorial Army, and was lucky enough to be chosen to be mobilised for the Gulf War. But that is another story.

Again I apologise for my violent dislike of the Argentine military and of Golden Balls. He was knighted. I am sure that made him happy. However, if this strange real-life story is ever to be useful to anyone else caught up by mistake in a violent war, it is probably as well that I should be as truthful and honest about my feelings as possible. Life is not always even, fair and organised, and we all sometimes have to work with difficult and unpleasant people, though probably few are as much so as I can be.

I do hope you have enjoyed this tale and will remember it mainly for the many fine acts of our Armed Forces in the conflict. I have certainly enjoyed writing it in our mountaintop retreat in North Cyprus, where the history of thousands of years of wars lies all around. With Yugoslavia, Sierra Leone and Ireland all in turmoil around us, I just wonder when the next war will catch some poor, unsuspecting general practitioner unawares. Be prepared!

Index